VICTORIAN ARCHITECTURE

VICTORIAN ARCHITECTURE
of Port Townsend Washington

Allen T. Denison
& Wallace K. Huntington

ISBN 0-88839-007-6

Copyright © 1978   ALLEN DENISON

Cataloging in Publication Data

Denison, Allen T., 1947—
    Victorian architecture of Port Townsend,
Washington

    Bibliography: p.
    ISBN 0-88839-007-6

    1. Port Townsend, Wash. - Buildings.
2. Architecture - Washington (State) - Port
Townsend. I. Huntington, Wallace Kay, 1926-
II. Title.
NA 735.P67D45   720'.9797'98   C78-002018-9

Published simultaneously in Canada and the United States by:

HANCOCK HOUSE PUBLISHERS LTD.
3215 Island View Road   SAANICHTON, B.C. V0S 1M0

HANCOCK HOUSE PUBLISHERS INC.
12008 1st Avenue South   SEATTLE, WA. 98168

Table of Contents

Glossary

ARCADE - a series of arches on columns applied to a wall or free standing.

ASHLAR - a wall surface of square or rectangular cut stones with uniform joints.

BALLOON FRAME - a structural system in wood architecture that uses light vertical, horizontal, and bracing members held together with nails.

BALUSTRADE - a decorative or functional railing consisting of regularly spaced vertical supports on a horizontal rail or series of lintels.

BARGE BOARD - the diagonal boards on the gable of a structure that follow directly under the roof. Often decorated.

BATTER - the slope on the sides of a wall when the wall is not truly vertical.

BELT COURSE - a decorative horizontal band that often articulates the various stories in a structure.

BRACKET - an elaborated projection from the wall that serves to physically or visually support a super-imposed weight, for example, a cornice.

CAPITAL - the top of a column on which the lintel rests; classically of three designs: doric, ionic, or corinthian.

COFFERED - a pattern on walls or ceiling of geometric recessed planes.

CORBEL - a projecting or cantilevered architectural form held in place by gravity. When used to bridge an opening, unlike the true arch, it needs no keystone.

CORNICE - a moulded projection which crowns or finishes the upper part of an architectural form. A part of the entablature that lies above the frieze.

CRESTING - a decorative treatment usually in wood or iron that crowns the ridge or peak of a roof.

DENTIL - a square block used in a series and connected by mouldings that form lineal decoration in cornices, etc.

ECLECTIC - in architecture, a random selection of styles or motifs assembled from various sources.

ENTABLATURE - in classic architecture, the area lying between the column capitals and the roof. It comprises the architrave, frieze, and cornice.

FEDERAL - a style of American architecture used in the late 18th and early 19th centuries, based on English Georgian architecture.

FENESTRATION - the arrangement and design of windows on a wall surface.

FRIEZE - a part of the entablature in a classical archi-tecture that features a running band of sculptured decorative elements.

GABLE - a roof structure of two sloping planes meeting at a ridge.

GOTHIC REVIVAL - a style of architecture of the late 18th and 19th centuries that re-interpreted gothic forms and proportions.

GREEK REVIVAL - an American architectural style of the first half of the 19th century based on classic Greek prototypes.

HIPPED ROOF - a roof structure that utilizes a sloping plane from each of the four walls of a house, thus avoiding a gable.

IMPOST BLOCK - the architectural form above the capital of a column from which the arch springs.

ITALIANATE - a 19th century style of architecture characterized by block-like forms capped with heavy cornices and usually having inconspicuous roofs.

LINTEL - a cross member or beam, usually above a door or window, supported by two side supports.

MANSARD ROOF - a type of roof invented in 17th century France that slopes or curves from the gutter line steeply upward to a horizontal plane.

MEDALLION - in architecture, a decorative geometric shape, round, oval, or polygonal, that has molded motifs in relief.

PATINATION or PATINA - a natural surface finish resulting from years of exposure to the elements.

PEDIMENT - that part of the entablature that is enclosed by the cornice. Usually a triangular shape that appears at the gable end of a classic building but may appear as a decorative feature over a window.

PILASTER - vertical columns or structural ribs that protrude from the surface of a wall and visually or structurally aids in a supporting function.

PORTICO - an entry porch that projects forward from a structure and is supported by columns.

ORGANIC - in architecture, forms that appear to be inspired from natural forms as opposed to purely geometric.

QUEEN ANNE - a late 19th century style of architec-ture in England and the United States that com-bined picturesque elements from various historical periods into a romantic and flexible new style of Victorian building.

QUOIN - the exterior corner of intersecting walls where there is usually a projecting plane that emphasizes the pattern of brick or stone.

RICHARDSON - an innovative 19th century American architect who revived Romanesque architecture to simplify forms and eliminate excess ornament. Important in the history of contem-porary architecture.

ROMANESQUE - pre-gothic architectural style that flourished in Europe in the 11th and 12th centuries. characterized by round arches and massive forms.

RUBBLE - a type of masonry featuring irregular shaped stones with uneven joints.

SASH - the frame that holds the glass in a window.

SEGMENTAL ARCH - an arch that isn't circular in its conformation but utilizes a segment of a curve.

SHEATHING - the continuous surface material on a structure that makes it weatherproof.

STICK-STYLE - a style of late Victorian architecture that was a reaction against applied decoration. It is characterized by its more functional appearance and frank expression of structural forms, for example, sheathing, panelling, bracing, and so forth.

TRUSS CONSTRUCTION - the use of spanning members that comprise a number of mutually dependent horizontals, verticals, and braces that allow for a longer and stronger support than a single beam.

TYMPANUM - the triangular area in a pediment that is enclosed by the raking (sloping) cornice and the horizontal cornice or the semi-circular area above the lintel of a door when the door is enclosed by an arch. Often an area for decoration.

VERNACULAR - in architecture, buildings that are not designed by professionals but are built from intuitive or natural instincts.

VILLA - in 19th century architecture, a detached house surrounded by landscaped grounds often in a rural context.

WAINSCOTTING - paneling that is applied to the lower part of interior walls.

WIDOW'S WALK - a flat roofed balustraded area on the roof of a house that traditionally allowed sea captains' wives to view the horizon for incoming ships.

Author's Notes & Acknowledgements

Some conversion and interpretation may be necessary to supplement information given in this book. Port Townsend's streets are not laid out north-south and east-west, but this book follows the convention set for many years, and assumes that Water Street runs east-west. Several prices are mentioned throughout the book which have little meaning without some basis for comparison. As a direct conversion of the consumer price index, a dollar in the years 1884-1893 can be multiplied by 3.7 to get 1967 dollars, or by approximately 6.7 for 1978. This rule doesn't work directly in all cases, however. Building costs were much lower then, as compared to real estate costs, a two-story house costing $1,800-$2,500. Materials were plentiful and labor was comparatively cheap. Some typical *daily* wages in the building industry were:

carpenters	$3.50 to $5 a day
plasterers	$5
house painters	$3.50
laborers and mill workers	$2

The photographs, unless otherwise noted, are current, and all the buildings exist as they are shown. The historical research relies heavily upon records and newspaper articles of the time.

Many people deserve thanks, but I will single out the staffs of the Jefferson County Historical Museum, Pioneer Title, the **Leader,** and the County Treasurer's office for being so tolerant and helpful.

It should be pointed out that Port Townsend is an actual, living town, not a museum like Williamsburg. Restoration has been done almost entirely with the owners' money and labor, and the homes are private residences. People are welcome to look at the houses from the street, but it should not be assumed that they are on tour unless otherwise noted. The owners would appreciate the consideration of respect for their privacy.

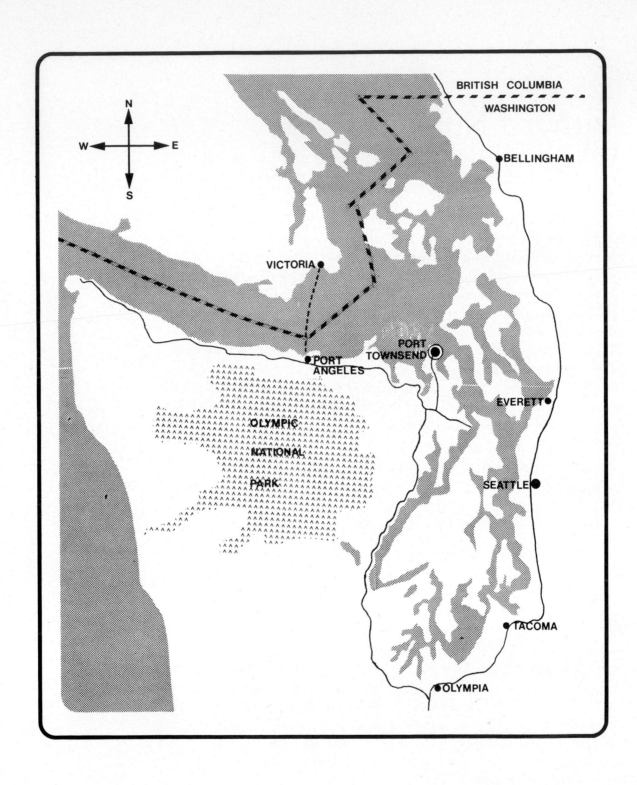

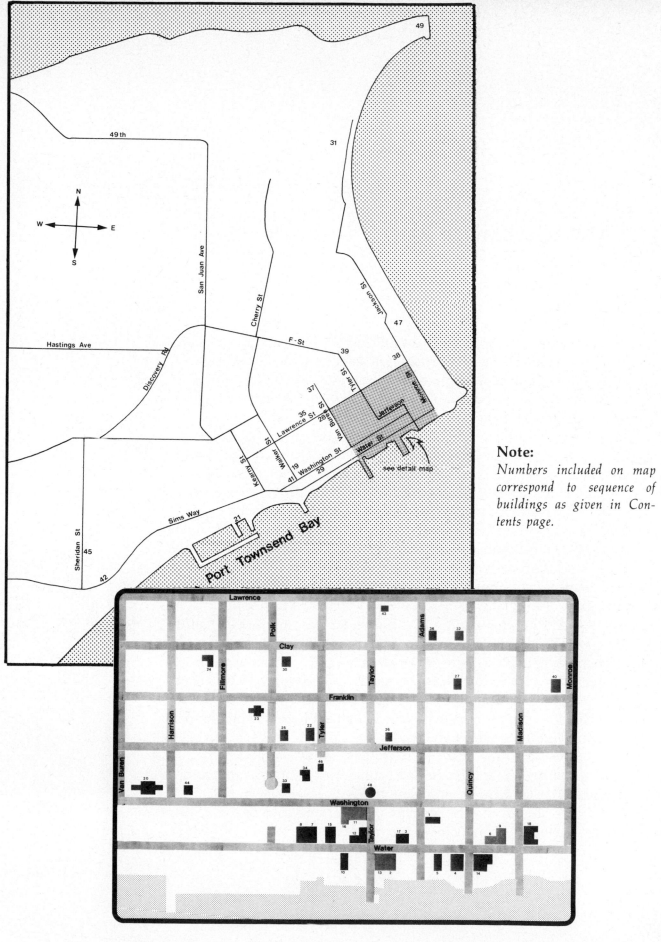

Note:
Numbers included on map correspond to sequence of buildings as given in Contents page.

Introduction and History

The treaty of 1846, which established the United States-Canadian border, precipitated an American expansion into the Puget Sound area. The reluctance of Americans to homestead in territory that might eventually be British had delayed this expansion, but the United States' bellicose sloganeering, "Fifty-four forty or fight," led to a reconciliation of the rival claims in time to take advantage of the disillusioned and restless adventurers from the California gold fields who had not "struck it rich." Because the area was relatively remote, the United States government allowed claims of 320 acres to a single citizen and 640 acres to a married man, a lucrative offer. San Francisco's rapid growth had created an insatiable demand for timber and agricultural products, both of which Puget Sound could readily furnish. Quick profits could be made by supplying this demand and even greater profit might accrue to the far-sighted if they could anticipate a site that would become the center of a future city.

Alfred Plummer and Charles Bachelder were advised by Capt. Lafayette Balch that Port Townsend had a good harbor and would be a fine place to stake a claim. After working in Steilacoom for the winter, the two men decided to do just that. Plummer staked a claim at Point Hudson, with Bachelder's claim adjacent. They were attracted by the vast timber resources and convenient harbor, and planned to supply San Francisco with lumber.

At the same time, F.W. Pettygrove, one of the founders of Portland, Oregon, and Loren B. Hastings yielded to that endemic restlessness so typical of settlers of the West. Hastings felt that Portland's climate and the presence of malaria were injurious to his family's health, and in October the two set out on foot for Olympia, then the largest city on Puget Sound. There they hired an Indian canoe

Alfred Plummer

10

and continued to Port Townsend. When they arrived, they saw that the site had more than trees and a harbor. There was good agricultural land, a good potential townsite, and several hundred Clallam and Chimacum Indians who had no trading post.

The two men returned to Portland where Hastings bought the sixty-foot pilot boat, *Mary Taylor.* They loaded it with merchandise for a store, their families, and various passengers. They arrived in Port Townsend on February 21, 1852, after eighteen days at sea.

The four pioneer families immediately formed a partnership for the purpose of fishing and trading. Their agreement included a clause which stated that any one of them could be bought out by the others if he drank to excess. This clause was almost immediately enforced against Bachelder, and Pettygrove bought his property for $300. (Bachelder moved to Port Ludlow and died shortly thereafter.) Bachelder had staked a claim, but hadn't filed it, so the three other men shifted their claims, so that Pettygrove was between Plummer and Hastings. Everything happened so fast that Bachelder's claim does not appear on the original claim map.

The three men agreed to donate equal shares of their claims for a townsite. It was laid out as far north as Lawrence Street. Plummer's part ran from Point Hudson to Tyler Street, Pettygrove's from Tyler to Walker, and Hastings's from Walker to the western city limit. With water on two sides and a bluff on the other, the site for the downtown was fine for shipping, but made adequate access difficult by land and complicated circulation between the sea-level business district and the elevated residential area. It was later thought that if the railroad were completed, the whole town would naturally expand to the south-west. The harbor was as good, the winds were gentler, and there was adequate room to expand.

The streets were laid out in line with the water, rather than in the compass directions the government preferred. This could have caused some problems had the town grown very large, as it did in Seattle where Arthur Denny laid out his streets the same way. Many streets were platted right over the bluff. Eventually they were graded to provide easier access between the residential district and downtown, and to provide fill dirt for the expanding downtown area.

By May 1852, there were three families and fifteen bachelors in Port Townsend. The growth and platting made the hundreds of local Indians restless. Their leader, Chetzemoka (or Cheech-ma-hun), called the "Duke of York" by the settlers, went to San Francisco that fall and was impressed by the huge city. He was convinced that the white men could not be stopped, and that coexistence was the best policy.

Chetzemoka Nov. 1873

Jefferson County Historical Society

11

The town applied for a post office and got it on September 28, 1852. This was propitious timing. A few months later Jefferson County was created out of Thurston County, and since Port Townsend was the only town with so much as a post office, it was named the county seat.

The Puget Sound Customs District had been created February 14, 1851, with Olympia as the port of entry, since it was virtually the only city on the Sound at the time. By August 1852, the customs collector, Simpson P. Moses, determined that Port Townsend would be a much better location for the port of entry. In 1853, Col. Isaac N. Ebey of Whidbey Island, was named collector, and the next year the customs headquarters were moved to Port Townsend. There were several reasons for this. Since ships had to make their first stop at the port of entry, Olympia was somewhat out of the way for most of them. Most ships passed by Port Townsend. It was also hard to suppress smuggling from the distant port of Olympia. Port Townsend, with a good harbor and lots of promise, was also considerably closer to Col. Ebey's home across the Sound. He could be signalled at his home and arrive at the customs office within an hour.

The customs headquarters provided Port Townsend with a distinct economic advantage. Since ships had to stop anyway, it became a logical distribution point. Ships' crews were paid off and ships resupplied there. In later years, the customs headquarters became the stabilizing factor in the economic base of the town, bringing in an annual income of four million dollars directly and another four million indirectly. This represented about $1,600 per person living in Port Townsend at the time, or roughly $10,000 in today's dollars.

TERMINAL DOCKS AND WAREHOUSES PORT TOWNSEND SOUTHERN RAILROAD.

From "Port Townsend Illustrated"

Several Indian uprisings discouraged settlement in Port Townsend. They climaxed with the beheading of Col. Ebey by the Kake Indians. A relative peace was attained by the end of the decade when the Fraser River gold rush brought a flood of prospectors to Puget Sound, most of whom needed food, lodging, and supplies for the rest of their journey.

In 1859, various Washington Territory cities were seeking Federal money for improvement projects. The city of Vancouver tried to form a block in the legislature with Port Townsend and Seattle. They planned that Vancouver would get the state capital, Seattle would get the territorial university, and Port Townsend would get the Federal penitentiary. They failed, and the capital remained at Olympia. Walla Walla got the penitentiary and Seattle ended up with the university. The Civil War brought more misfortune to the area. Supplies arrived erratically and prices rose, discouraging business and growth.

The worst blow to the town was the removal of the customs house. Morris Frost, the customs collector, had constructed a two-story brick custom building. But after Abraham Lincoln was elected, he appointed Victor Smith as collector. Smith was temporarily in the east where he had access to Washington, D.C. He lobbied to have the custom house moved to Port Angeles, where he had extensive real estate holdings, and his request was granted on June 19, 1862. Returning to the west coast, he demanded that Port Townsend surrender the customs records in the new brick building, or he would level the town with the twelve-pounders aboard the steamer *Shubrick*. Faced with such an unpalatable alternative, the townspeople surrendered the records. In 1863, a reservoir in Port Angeles broke and Smith's custom house was swept out to sea, though some of the records were salvaged by Makah Indians. Smith drowned in 1865, and the custom house was brought back to Port Townsend the next year.

In the early 1870s, rumors of a railroad coming to Puget Sound from Portland, via Kalama, initiated enthusiastic self-promotion among the rival cities, but the Northern Pacific decided to locate its terminus at Tacoma, which, at that time, had a population of approximately zero. In response, nearly every town on the Sound planned to build its own railroad to Portland, which then had a population of about 25,000. Port Townsend was no exception. However, these plans were abandoned when Jay Cooke, a large banking firm, went bankrupt and triggered a severe nationwide depression. Port Townsend's economy survived the ensuing years mostly because of the custom house, which did four times the business that Portland's custom house did.

By the 1880s there was renewed prosperity, and the large Bartlett Building was constructed in Port Townsend in 1881. Transcontinental railroad service reached Tacoma in 1883 and its promise of opening Puget Sound to increased trade started a land boom which, though slowed by another brief depression, peaked in 1889.

By the late 1880s Port Townsend was still a city of the future, and still fighting an uphill battle with other cities on the Sound. Around 1870, the populations of Seattle, Olympia, and Port Townsend were each about 1,000, and Tacoma didn't exist. But by 1890, Seattle and Tacoma both had more than 35,000 residents, and Port Townsend was far behind with only 4,565, although they claimed 6,000. How did Port Townsend slip so far behind the other cities?

Apparently, the citizens of Port Townsend were so confident that they didn't bother to encourage investment. They felt that their natural resources and advantageous location made success inevitable for the town. At the same time that Seattle was giving land to new industries, Port Townsend was maintaining high real estate prices. As one man commented, "Fowler asked as much for a little strip of the gravel beach as he would have to pay for a thirty-acre lot in the kingdom of heaven."[1] So new industries preferred to locate in other cities. In 1889, the **Morning Leader** said in retrospect:

. . . in years gone by Port Townsend has suffered severely from lack of the push and energy that has made Seattle the metropolis of Washington. Money was too easily made and our businessmen

THE WEST SHORE

FROM THE MARINE HOSPITAL

Along the Wharves.

PORT TOWNSEND.

became indifferent to the gradual encroachment of the energetic cities near the head of tide-water. Not until this city was threatened with a loss of the Puget Sound customs district headquarters did our businessmen become thoroughly awakened to the seriousness of the situation. Only as far back as the beginning of 1885, the editor of this paper remembers the language of gentlemen forecasting a dismal future for this city. A few men openly talked of commercial disruption and refused to put their money in substantial brick buildings. But a few years have wrought great changes. A handful of enterprising men of small capital engaged in steamboating . . . and drove out competition. They made easy money because the town was so ideally situated, the businessmen woke up and built brick buildings . . .

It seems difficult now to imagine Port Townsend as a huge commercial center, but the idea was plausible at the time. There were a variety of natural resources: a sandstone quarry, iron, coal, timber, good agricultural land, and fish, among others. These fed the local enterprises, including the only iron furnace in the territory at Irondale, sawmills, wood products factories, and a resort for tourists and sportsmen.[3]

WATER STREET LOOKING EAST.

From "Port Townsend Illustrated"

Of primary importance, though, was the harbor. A **Morning Leader** article claimed that Port Townsend was actually 700 miles closer to Liverpool than San Francisco, since the ships had to sail so far north to catch the currents to San Francisco. Captains liked to sail along latitudinal lines, such as in the Straits of Juan de Fuca, which could be entered in any wind. Also, ships could avoid towage fees of $400-$900 to other points in the Sound. All these factors were minimized by the steamboats which were quickly replacing the sailing vessels.

According to the **Morning Leader**, the harbor covered fifty square miles and had an even clay bottom with an average depth of ten fathoms, which was excellent for an anchorage. The harbors in both Tacoma and Seattle were too deep for anchoring, although this problem could be circumvented by the use of docks.[4] Also, the custom house was located in Port Townsend, which still meant that all vessels had to stop there. Even though it was the second busiest port of entry in the United States (only New York registered more tonnage), most ships did not unload in Port Townsend because it was not a population center. Since it was without a railroad, it was not a good distribution point. Also, it was on a peninsula, which hindered shipping to and from the east, though there was some consolation in knowing that San Francisco was also on a peninsula.

A railroad was the greatest economic blessing that any nineteenth-century town could have, and in 1887 the Port Townsend Southern Railroad was formed to provide a rail connection to Portland. On March 23, 1889 work started, and the town had a large celebration. After one mile was cleared, work stopped. The towns-people hoped that a large company would become interested in the plan. Late in 1889, Union Pacific announced that it intended to make Port Townsend the western terminus of its system, and optimism ran high.[5] The next February, Charles Eisenbeis negotiated a contract with H.W. McNeill of the Oregon Improvement Company, which was closely associated with Union Pacific.[6]

On March 12, 1890, the contract was signed; the Oregon Improvement Company would build a railroad and provide rail service to Portland. In return, Port Townsend would grant the franchise, raise a bonus of $100,000, and donate extensive real estate to the Oregon Improvement Company. The $100,000 was raised in three days. The land, including more than fifty acres donated by Lucinda Hastings for the terminal grounds, was transferred. The Oregon Improvement Company promised to lay twenty miles of track by the end of June, at a cost of half a million dollars, and to provide employment for 1,500 men. At the same time, the company started selling off much of the land which had been donated to it for the terminal. A large business district was planned with San Juan Avenue and Lawrence Street as the main thoroughfares. If the land had been sold it would have resulted in a profit of more than $1.2 million, without even including the land that had been donated as a rail right-of-way.[8]

Anticipation of a railroad engendered frantic real estate speculation. Several brick buildings were constructed during the summer of 1889, and most of the space was leased before the buildings were completed. The town claimed more brick buildings than any town of its size in Washington. Prosperity had finally arrived, and the **Morning Leader** issued the statement which seems ironic today:

A few of the old landmarks remain, but these are rapidly giving place to a new and more substantial class of buildings. Unlike many of the cities of the West now undergoing this rapid and undreamed of transformation, Port Townsend has but few, if, in fact, any, of that class of citizens whose proverbial "first love" for the old haunts of former days is permitted to dominate over their ambition to see a new and more prosperous town.[9]

From "Port Townsend Illustrated"

Those people were referred to as "mossbacks," and it was the **Leader**'s opinion that "the busy world will gather more life and revolve more smoothly when they are gone."[10] In a later article, it stated that, "This city is on the eve of a greater 'boom,' if we may be permitted to use that objectionable word, than has ever visited Puget Sound."[11]

Indicating the activity of the time, real estate transactions ror the thirty-seven year period from 1851 through 1887 fill seven volumes of record books, but just four years - 1888 through 1891 - fill thirteen volumes, roughly seventeen times the previous pace. On one day, after the railroad contract was signed, $250,000 in real estate was transferred.

The prosperity brought in large numbers of people, and the population of the area reached a peak of about 7,000. The town's facilities were stretched, and many people boarded in houses or in the hotels which had been quickly converted into boarding houses. Unfortunately, good times also made the town more raucous. Sailors who spent their wages in town while waiting to sign on another ship, and many shiftless or idle drifters, gave the town a notorious reputation. The downtown area became even rougher, particularly the east end of Water Street. Fighting and shanghaiing were common. Smuggling of opium to avoid the twelve-dollar-per-pound duty, and importation of Chinese laborers, in violation of the Chinese Exclusion Act, were rampant. The east end of town was the home of many of the Chinese, and the location of the worst of approximately fifty saloons in town. It was also the site of at least twelve businesses which the 1891 fire map tactfully refers to as "female boarding" houses. The **Leader** pleaded with the police to close down three Siwash (Indian) brothels on the charge of serving liquor to Indians, but the paper didn't comment on the other brothels.[12] It reported on the sentencing of a petty thief with a long record to sixty days in the county jail, after which he was to be shipped as a sailor on board some vessel bound for the cholera-infested parts of Japan.[13]

The prosperity also increased the fierce competition among Puget Sound cities. They were all striving to be bigger and better at everything. High tax assessments were a sign of status. When fire burned most of downtown Seattle to the ground in 1889, the citizens of Port Townsend undoubtedly considered the disaster a boon to their own commerce. Although Seattle and Tacoma were much larger, Port Townsend was insulted that the 1890 census only credited the town with 4,565 rather than 6,000 citizens. The citizens realized that the large population living just north of the Lawrence Street city limit was not being counted. Too late, they expanded their city limits to increase the population and physical size of the town.

The many newspapers on the Sound were not above printing "falsehoods, of the silliest nature,"[14] about other towns in order to discourage new settlers. When Seattle claimed that it was the terminus of the Union Pacific Railroad shortly after Port Townsend had made the same claim, the **Leader** responded, "This will cause no surprise among persons who have grown accustomed to her usual bluster."[15] In order to rectify any false images, the **Leader** planned to issue a promotional publication, **Port Townsend Illustrated,** which would spread the "truth" about Port Townsend to the rest of the world. When Nellie Bly completed her trip around the world in seventy-two days, Port Townsend planned to send Regina Rothschild, the daughter of D.C.H. Rothschild, around the world in fifty-seven days in order to show Port Townsend's shipping advantages, but the trip never took place.[16]

Hotel Eisenbeis   *From "Port Townsend Illustrated"*

The desire of local citizens for a "first class" tourist hotel must have rankled the owners of existing hotels. Charles Eisenbeis intended to put a hotel in his planned Mount Baker Block. Other promoters wanted a hotel like the Rainier in Seattle. In fact, they wanted it identical to the Rainier.[17] They estimated that it would raise property values by 30% and could be built in 100 days, in time for the 1890 tourist season. They needed $50,000 and raised $20,000 in half an hour. Even Eisenbeis subscribed to the new hotel. The plan faltered, and various alternatives were proposed. Eisenbeis offered to build a $35,000 hotel at the west end of town, if a $10,000 bonus could be raised. Also for $10,000, Capt. Tibbals and F.W. Pettygrove Jr. offered to add two stories to their new buildings and make them into a "first-class" hotel. In March 1890, shortly after the railroad contract was signed and the $100,000 bonus assured, the Port Townsend Southern Railroad and its general manager, H.W. McNeill, announced their plans to build a $100,000 hotel overlooking the railroad terminal. This plan apparently fizzled, although a three-story frame hotel, costing probably less than $10,000 was built on the terminal grounds and named the Hotel McNeill. The "first-class" hotel, the Hotel Eisenbeis, was finally built by an offshoot of the Big Five Syndicate (R.C. Hill, Henry Landes, J.A. Kuhn, Thomas Jackman, and Charles Eisenbeis), called the Port Townsend Hotel and Improvement Company. J.A. Kuhn served as president, in spite of the fact that he was building a huge hotel downtown. The Hotel Eisenbeis was similar to the Rainier, designed by the same architects, Saunders and Houghton. It had 138 rooms, all the "first-class" amenities, and was located on the hill, in the Syndicate's Eisenbeis addition, over-looking the railroad terminal. It was finished in August 1890, but nobody would lease it. This prompted the January 1, 1891 **Leader** to comment, "Although prematurely built, it will someday prove a valuable investment."[18] Sixteen years later, it was finally occupied as a sanitarium. It eventually burned down.

The fate of the hotel is typical of the time. The optimism and building activity were blunted by tight money during the summer of 1890. Besides the hotel and a Catholic hospital west of town, the only major private construction consisted of two $100,000 buildings erected downtown by Charles Eisenbeis and Joe Kuhn. Neither was ever completely finished. In the fall, the future looked dim, but the **Leader** optimistically reported, at slightly inflated prices:
Millions of dollars have been put in substantial residences and business blocks. Among those most notable, either completed or in process of construction are a dozen houses costing $10,000 to $200,000 each, a $125,000 hotel, a $110,000 hospital, a $250,000 custom house, a $100,000 courthouse, a $50,000 school, and on the

railway terminal grounds $500,000 has been and is being spent.[19]

In November, Baring Brothers, a large financial house which held many American railroad contracts, was rumored to be failing, and there were many management changes within several railroad companies. On November 25, 1890, the Oregon Improvement Company went into receivership. It was unable to pay the interest due December 1. The **Leader,** a paragon of optimism, reported on the 26th that the Oregon Improvement Company embarrassment was only temporary, and would be cleared up in sixty days, but the next day, Thanksgiving, it said, bitterly:

. . . a policy has been pursued that gives us very little better railroad facilities, and the temporary disadvantage of being involved, to a certain extent, in the financial complications of a company that never expected to use our line for other purpose than to promote a general scheme of railroad construction and townsite speculation.[20]

This was obviously a serious setback to the town's plans. If the rails had been completed, Port Townsend would probably have had rail service despite the company's insolvency, but the rails got only as far as Quilcene, and the dream of transcontinental railroad service died with the company. Amidst the gloom, **Port Townsend Illustrated** was issued on December 7 showing the promise that had almost become reality.

J.A. Kuhn, 1899

PORT ✻ TOWNSEND

✻ ITS ✻ ADVANTAGES ✻ RESOURCES ✻ AND ✻
PROPSECTS

HANDSOMELY
ILLUSTRATED

Entered according to Act of Congress, in the year 1890, by the Leader Publishing Company, in the office of the Librarian of Congress, at Washington.

PUBLISHED BY THE
LEADER PUBLISHING COMPANY.
J. E. CLARKE, Manager.

Title page from "Port Townsend Illustrated"

The bankruptcy of the railroad and the national depression of 1893 led to an exodus of a significant part of the population. Most of them went to Seattle. The 2,000 remaining clung to the hope of the still present customs headquarters, the natural resources, and a diminished but still extant hope of a future rail connection. A drydock and nail factory were planned and later built. Through the years various minor industries, such as fishing and canning, kept the town going. The military built a new marine hospital, an army post at Fort Worden, and a coast guard station.

However, various subports of entry were established throughout Puget Sound, eroding the influence of Port Townsend's most important asset, and the customs headquarters was moved to Seattle in 1911. There was little demand for housing, and, since the city was planned for 20,000, there was plenty of room to build a new house or building without going through the effort of tearing down an old one. The town led a slow somnolent existence which prompted one reference to it as the "world's only lighted cemetery."[21] In 1927, the Crown Zellerbach mill was built and this stabilized the town's economy but did not change its appearance.

Following World War II, a national era of massive demolition and shoddy reconstruction was nearly as destructive of historic values in American cities as the war had been to European cities. Port Townsend, benefiting from benign neglect, survived remarkably intact. It lost a few structures to fire and others to "modernization," but retained the essential quality of a late Victorian seacoast town.

The 1960s brought a renewed interest in Victorian architecture, and formerly apathetic owners started to restore and preserve buildings, generally with their own money and skills. Today, with much work done but more left to do, the Victorian flavor of the town can easily be appreciated. The downtown area of 1890 is still the downtown area. The population is still around 5,000, so there has been little pressure to move or tear down the central business district, as has been done in other cities. The town is still somewhat confined by the bluff and the water, although access has been improved. There are no skyscrapers to destroy the scale of the business district. The area functions as a town rather than a museum or false-fronted tourist mecca.

Discounting both historic bias and romanticism, most critics must conclude that American communities of the nineteenth century were physically more attractive than those of the twentieth century. The uniformity of scale, continuity of materials, and cohesiveness of structure in Victorian towns was sacrificed to expediency in the age of the automobile. Both the ineffable charm and the tangible physical attributes of nineteenth century American towns have largely disappeared. By a quirk of fate, Port Townsend has retained an extremely large proportion of its Victorian structures. The typical evolution that expanding twentieth century cities followed—burgeoning business districts eroding the once contiguous residential property —did not occur in Port Townsend due to the unique physical barriers that separated the residential and commercial areas. This topographical distinction and the sudden economic plunge in the last decade of the nineteenth century are responsible for the existence of this historic anachronism. Other Victorian seacoast towns have survived - Cape May, New Jersey and Galveston, Texas, are especially notable - but Port Townsend, Washington, remains the finest example of a Victorian seacoast town on the west coast.

1. **Puget Sound Weekly Argus,** December 27, 1883 "Reminiscences of Port Townsend, by James G. Swan
2. **Morning Leader,** November 2, 1889
3. **West Shore,** May 1885
4. **Morning Leader,** June 29, 1890, February 14, 1890
5. **Morning Leader,** December 7, 1889, October 12, 1889
6. **Morning Leader,** February 14, 1890
7. **Morning Leader,** March 3, 1890
8. **Morning Leader,** May 15, 1890
9. **Morning Leader,** January 1, 1890
10. **Morning Leader,** February 9, 1890
11. **Morning Leader,** February 23, 1890
12. **Morning Leader,** May 11, 1890
13. **Morning Leader,** October 18, 1890
14. **Morning Leader,** December 12, 1889
15. **Morning Leader,** December 8, 1889
16. **Morning Leader,** March 23, 1890
17. **Morning Leader,** December 24, 1889
18. **Morning Leader,** January 1, 1891
19. **Morning Leader,** October 25, 1890
20. **Morning Leader,** November 27, 1890
21. **The Egg and I,** Betty MacDonald, p. 57

Fowler Building

Bartlett Building-1881

C.C. Bartlett

C.C. Bartlett and Company was one of the first large general merchandise businesses on Puget Sound. Charles C. Bartlett arrived from Maine in 1864 and operated a hotel for two years. He then bought a store from Francis W. James which he sold five years later. In 1881 he bought the Hastings Brothers' store. That same year he built Bartlett's Stone Block (as it was called) on the same site, to accommodate his business. For years it was the largest and most substantial building in town, doing an extensive business in general merchandise, shipping and commission, wines, liquors, and ship chandlery: providing a wholesale and retail outlet for Alaska and Puget Sound. Charles left the company in the hands of his son, Frank A. Bartlett, and his brother, F. Albert Bartlett, while he went to Juneau to operate a trading post and cannery. When he returned in 1888 the population of the town had soared and many other substantial buildings were being planned. Bartlett borrowed large sums of money to invest in the future of the town, but his health was declining and he died in Los Angeles in 1893 at the age of fifty-five. The estate was immediately beseiged by creditors, and the company was eventually dissolved, though the Bartlett family continued to operate a men's furnishings store in the same location for many years.

Though only the second story of the Bartlett Building remains intact, the Victorian elegance of the window proportions and the almost Federal restraint in decorative detail make this handsome structure a perfect foil for the more exuberant architecture of the following decades. The sandstone of which it is constructed was probably from the quarry at Scow Bay between Indian Island and Marrowstone Island. It communicates the particularly satisfying sense of weight that is inherent in stone construction.

C.C. Bartlett Building, Water St.

First National Bank Building-1883

Henry Landes opened a small office in 1879 which was the first financial institution in Port Townsend. By 1883 there was sufficient demand for him to open the First National Bank with capital stock of $50,000. The $7,000 building, on the site of F.W. James' store, was originally one story. The brick second story was probably added in 1885. Landes received support mainly from San Francisco and from Robert C. Hill, who had recently settled in Port Townsend and who became cashier of the bank. Since it was the only bank in Jefferson, Clallam, Island, and San Juan counties at the time, it enjoyed a large patronage. It was one of two banks in Port Townsend that survived the depression of the 1890s.

The vicissitudes of time are apparent in the surviving parts of the First National Bank. The arbitrary change of materials from stone on the ground floor to brick on the second floor is still an enigma, however. Although the building survives as a fragment, the second story facade with crisp delineated corners, a nicely proportioned cornice, and ornamented window entablatures are evidence of an architectural sophistication in Port Townsend at an early stage of its development.

First National Bank Building, Water St.

Waterman and Katz Building-1885

Adele & Israel Katz

Sigmund Waterman and Soloman Katz arrived from San Francisco in 1861 and immediately opened a store on Water Street. Ten years later they moved into larger quarters on Lawrence Street. Their store became known as "Solomon's Temple" and the area was called "Katzville." When Katz died in 1879 his interest was bought out by William and Israel Katz. In 1885, the store was moved into even larger quarters in this $20,000 building downtown. Waterman died of rheumatism in San Francisco in 1888. In the same year, William Katz was killed while attempting to sail his boat across the bow of the *Palmyra,* a much larger vessel. The two boats collided and the Katz boat was cut in two. William Katz drowned, leaving Israel the sole owner of the store, by then the third largest in the territory. He continued to operate the store for about twenty-five years and was elected mayor in 1915. He served for two years, but mysteriously disappeared shortly thereafter.

The large building was entirely occupied by Waterman and Katz's business. There were some rooms for employees, but most of the space was devoted to merchandise, including carpets, furniture, liquor, and Indian goods, which were sold to tourists. They did so much wholesale and retail business that they had to build a large warehouse to the rear of the store in 1887 and another addition in 1889.

The severely handsome three-story brick structure with stone quoining and sills has an elegantly bracketed cornice and original iron roof cresting. The closely spaced windows with corbelled brick entablatures give a maximum amount of light to the interior as well as establishing the pleasing rhythm of the second and third story arcades. The subdued decorative scheme enhances the subtle use of brick in dentiled cornice bands and recessed panels and lends an unexpected simplicity in a period when Victorian excesses predominated.

Waterman and Katz Building, Water St.

Waterman and Katz Building

Side of Waterman & Katz Bldg.

C.F. Clapp Building - 1885

C.F. Clapp, 1872

"The Honorable Cyrus F. Clapp, Capitalist," as he was listed in the Port Townsend Directory of 1897, is shown in an early photograph dressed in natty clothes and posed with a dashing air, in contrast to the usual dour and stiff poses of the town's businessmen.

Mrs. Clapp also had style and became a town legend when she gave an afternoon party with electric lights aglow. Electricity at the time was a luxury only few could afford and available only in the evening. The special firing-up of the generators for this show of opulence reputedly cost her husband $75.00.

Clapp was born in Maine, attended Hanover Academy in Massachusetts, the Royal Institute in Belfast and Saint Andrews College in Scotland, returning home in 1868 at the age of seventeen. He arrived in Port Townsend in 1870 with $5.00 in his pocket to work for his uncle at the Cosmopolitan Hotel. Six years later, aged twenty-five, he purchased the hotel. He subsequently sold it, became a merchant in Dungeness, and built this $13,000 building, one of the earlier "substantial" buildings in the city. The original tenant in 1885, Peyser Brothers Dry Goods, was replaced by the Merchants Bank, which Clapp and J.H. Feuerbach established in 1887. (It was sold in 1889 to William Ladd of the Ladd and Tilton Bank in Portland and moved the following year to the Mount Baker Block.) Various saloons operated in the building during the early decades. Originally in the basement, they later occupied the first floor.

The cast iron facade of the Clapp Building, applied on a plastered brick face, predates the facades by the Port Townsend Foundry which was having organizational trouble at the time. It was cast by Washington Iron Works in Seattle. However, the iron itself

C.F. Clapp Building, Water St.

undoubtedly came from Irondale, euphemistically called "a manufacturing suburb of Port Townsend" which was the only smelting works in the state at the time. (It had been in operation since 1878.) Though the delicately detailed frieze above the street level windows is a later addition and introduces a horizontal division disproportionate to the original conception, the building is largely intact, and is one of the truly fine cast iron facades in the Puget Sound area. The stilted segmental (or straight sided) arch that is used on the upper story had appeared in England as early as 1848 but in American architecture it flourished but briefly as a significant feature of High Victorian Italianate. The straight "legs" of the arch, which rise from the impost block, lack any structural logic, but its iconoclastic defiance of the orders made it particularly popular as a decorative feature in American vernacular architecture. The pilasters that form the pleasing vertical divisions of the structure engage and lend a visual support to the massive cornice, giving an organic coherence to the total fabric of the facade.

Franklin House-1886

Dave Spoor, 1874

This building, the first brick hotel in town, was built by David Spoor, a New Yorker who, like many of Port Townsend's early settlers, had been an unsuccessful miner in California and British Columbia. He became a builder in 1869 and did the initial construction of the Central Hotel in 1875. In 1877 Spoor bought the Franklin House from J.J. Hunt, who took over the management of the Cosmopolitan Hotel. Spoor built a new hotel building in 1886, and for three years the Franklin House claimed the distinction of being "the only fireproof brick hotel in the city," despite the fact that the rear two-thirds was wood. Its main competition came from the Central and Cosmopolitan, both of which were built of wood. In 1889 many brick buildings were constructed, including the Clarendon Hotel next door. At this time, the Franklin House was occupied by several boarders, a common occurrence due to the sudden increase in the population of the town.

Spare and without artifice, this building seems to have resulted from a collaboration between brick mason and carpenter. Certainly the whimsical lack of coordination between the openings on the ground floor and those above seem the result of casual planning. Contemporary structures of the period, by comparison, seem obsessive about articulating the floors on the exterior and filling wall spaces with ornament, whereas in this vernacular structure economy and function predominate over fashion.

Franklin House, Water St.

Capt. Tibbals Building - 1889

architects: Whiteway and Schroeder

Capt. Tibbals (see also Tibbals house, page 102) erected this $28,000 building shortly before his retirement, using the money he had accumulated in a long and prosperous life in Port Townsend. It was originally planned to provide store space on the main floor and offices above, but changes were made to accommodate local demands. Instead, the main floor housed three saloons and the upstairs was occupied by real estate offices and The Tacoma, a rooming house. At one time Tibbals and F.W. Pettygrove, Jr., who owned the Pioneer Building next door, considered adding a story to both their buildings and making them into one large "first-class" hotel, but the idea was abandoned when plans for the Hotel Eisenbeis started to take shape.

The year 1889 was one of intense building activity and optimism in Port Townsend. The **Morning Leader** of November 31, 1889, commenting on Capt. Tibbals's sixty-fourth birthday celebration, added, "Captain Tibbals is among Port Townsend's earliest residents, and intends staying with the city until it has acquired a population of 100,000 prosperous citizens."

The building today, except for the missing cornice, looks much as it did in the 1890 lithograph published in **Port Townsend Illustrated.** Whiteway and Schroeder, the architects, planned many of Port Townsend's distinctive buildings. This is one of their most progressive designs. Using a Richardsonian style of Romanesque derivation, the architects grouped the windows in the three-story structure into large-scale arched bays that rise from a more massive first floor that, capped by a straightforward and undecorated cornice, serves as a podium for

Capt. Tibbals Building, Water and Tyler Sts.

41

the two upper floors. The attenuated pilasters that serve to visually support the arches are a complexity of form and material derived from earlier Victorian sources and they negate some of the vitality and strength of the conception. Despite this, the building established a new standard of "modern" design for Port Townsend at the time of its completion.

Exterior detail Capt. Tibbals Bldg.

Pioneer Building-1889

architects: Whiteway and Schroeder

The Pioneer Building, like many others built around 1890, proved to be a bad investment for its builders. It was a joint venture by Francis W. Pettygrove, Jr., son of one of Port Townsend's founders, and the State Bank of Washington. The November 24, 1889 **Morning Leader** describes the Bank's half (west side) as:

. . . costing $28,000. The building is 27x90 feet, three stories high. The first story is cut stone—solid rock; the remainder of the front is artificial stone. It will be fire-proof throughout and one of the best finished buildings north of San Francisco, with plate glass front and finished in natural wood . . . The second and third floors of the building contain sixteen rooms and offices, all of which are now leased for a term of three years.

Pettygrove's half was similar, and the ground floor was occupied by John Iffland's Boca Saloon.

Pettygrove was a grocer who sold his business on October 3, 1889 to Jarrett T. Lewis (see Hastings Building, page 56) and went to Pasadena for a winter vacation while his building was being finished. At the time, his estimated worth was $140,000. Despite this, two lumber companies issued liens against his building, and he took two mortgages totalling $18,000, neither of which was satisfied. As a result, the First National Bank foreclosed and became the owner in 1893.

The January 26, 1890 **Morning Leader** reported:

The State Bank of Washington will open next Saturday, February 1, in its new brick and stone building on Water Street. The capital stock of this bank is $75,000 and its officers are: D.W. Smith president; Wm. Payne, vice-president; Chas. A. Dyer, cashier; Chas. P. Swiggert,

Pioneer Building, Water St.

assistant cashier. The interior of the bank has been elegantly fitted up at an expense of nearly $25,000, all of the fixtures coming from Cincinnati (costing $15,000). The counter is of an artistic design, entirely different from any other in the city, and has a fine marble foot-board its full length. The vault is 8 x 12 feet, with air chambers running through its walls, and is entirely fire-proof. It is set on nine feet of solid masonry, and holds nicely arranged shelves and cabinets. The safe is of the McNeale & Urban make and weighs 4800 pounds. The directors of the State Bank of Washington have every assurance of success.

Three years later they sold out to the Bank of California, who quietly closed the doors shortly thereafter.

Architects Whiteway and Schroeder's extensive practice in Port Townsend gives the architectural student some indication of the ambiguity of style in professional architect's offices in the late nine-teenth century. Commitment to the more progressive Richardsonian style shown in the Captain Tibbals building is absent in the Pioneer Building. Though using the more "modern" artificial cast stone in preference to natural stone, the building is conservative, perhaps in deference to the wishes of the client. It is the least cohesive design by this firm, which in this instance failed to bring any conviction to the use of the assorted materials: brick, stone, iron, and wood. The pattern of fenestration is a normal Victorian development, using horizontal lintels on the first floor, segmental arched openings on the second, and circular arched openings on the third. But the complex and arbitrary changes of material destroy the potential harmony of the arcading and the disruptive central vertical division on the second and third floor, necessitated by the dual ownership, caused a disturbing break in rhythm. The Victorian tolerance for complexity of form and pattern can be justified as a cultural bias in many instances, but the Pioneer Building, heavy-handed at best, is more interesting in its parts than as a successful design.

Fowler-Caines Block - 1889

architects: Whiteway and Schroeder

Originally the Clarendon Hotel, this building was constructed for Mary Fowler, widow of Capt. E.S. Fowler, and Robert M. Caines, her son, at a cost of $18,000. The opening of the Clarendon was a grand event described as follows in the December 17, 1889 issue of the **Morning Leader**:

The new Clarendon hotel and bar was opened last night, and proved one of the most brilliant affairs of the kind ever held in this city. The large bar and billiard room was crowded nearly all evening, and a jolly time was had by all present. The **Morning Leader** *office acknowledges the receipt of a handsome compliment in the shape of several bottles of Pommery Sec.*

Five days later the **Leader** reported:

There are 34 rooms in the hotel, all hard finished, carpeted, well lighted with the rays of the sunlight through the day and with electricity at night, and the outside rooms are provided with stoves. All the rooms are provided with electric call bells, which connect with the office. The ladies' parlor is on the second floor, and is fitted up in the most approved style. All the furniture is upholstered, and is of the best quality. The office, on the ground floor, is very large and nicely arranged. The sample rooms, off of the office, are very large and well appointed and cannot fail to be appreciated by commercial travellers. Everything about the hotel appears metropolitan. The bar and billiard room is a model. All the fixtures are expensive in themselves, and no expense has been spared in arranging them in a neat tasty manner in the room. Mr. Wm. Cartwright has charge of the barroom, where he officiates with his customary grace, and few men in the city have more friends. Taken altogether the Clarendon Hotel is a credit to the city.

Fowler-Caines Block, Water and Madison Sts.

47

Fred Lewis bought the building in 1934, changed the sign on the front, and operated his emporium there.

The Fowler-Caines Block is the most pleasing of the numerous structures known to be designed by the firm of Whiteway and Schroeder. Conservative in its use of materials—brick construction with applied cast iron columns from the Port Townsend Foundry on the ground floor—it has a forthrightness and lack of affectation that are missing in the firm's more "modern" Romanesque designs.

By projecting the center section of the building slightly forward in the second and third stories and cornice, there is a tripartite division vertically to match the three horizontal divisions. The second- and third-story windows also fall into patterns of three in each of the geometric divisions with alternating narrow and wide apertures. The consistency and harmony of this fenestration, plus the fine quality of brickwork and the pleasingly scaled bracketed cornice, give this structure a restrained sophistication not matched by other structures in the two-year period preceding the Depression.

Side of Fowler – Caines Block

Sterming Block - 1889

architects: Whiteway and Schroeder

George J. Sterming had been a long-time saloon keeper in Port Townsend when he built the $12,000 Sterming Block to house his popular Belmont Restaurant and Saloon. The upstairs held a variety of offices, including those of the Key City Building and Loan Association, with J.C. Saunders as president, and those of Port Townsend's most prolific architects, Whiteway and Schroeder.

The double projecting bay facade was a specialty in Port Townsend (three are extant and an earlier wood prototype, the Adams Block, is pictured in **Port Townsend Illustrated**). This well-preserved building by architects Whiteway and Schroeder is the most successful example of a difficult genre of commercial structures. Though not completely overcoming the problem of making such buildings look like a single facade rather than two adjacent underscale buildings, there is a harmony between the parts of this structure not apparent in the others. The cast iron pilasters by the Port Townsend Foundry are carried through the second story in brick, forming a visual continuity and support to the cornice. The decorative coffered band that extends across the base of the bays is integrated into the structural lines of the facade. The proportions and scale as well as the texture of the locally manufactured brick give the Sterming Block a sophistication and harmony less evident in the Terry Building or Siebenbaum Building.

Miller and Burkett Block - 1889

architects: Whiteway and Schroeder

B.S. Miller and H.L. Burkett obtained a twenty-five-year lease on this property in return for $800 a year and a promise to erect a building of stone, brick, and iron. Their $18,000 venture proved unsuccessful. Several liens were brought against them almost as soon as the building was completed, and they eventually forfeited the building and their lease to satisfy the mortgage.

The ground floor was used as a liquor store and the short-lived Key City Club was upstairs. After serving as a meeting place for other clubs, the Elks bought the building in 1905 and have been there ever since.

The prolific Whiteway and Schroeder worked in their accustomed Romanesque style here. They used Port Townsend Foundry iron columns on the street level and combined brick and cast stone on the upper stories and tower. Here again, by extending the pilasters of the ground floor up through the second and third stories, the windows are divided into sets of three, giving an orderly if somewhat massive appearance. Whiteway and Schroeder were rarely generous in the sizing of windows or the extent of glass in relation to masonry and here, as in other of their commercial structures, a solemn monumentality results.

Sterming Block, Water St.

Miller and Burkett Block, Washington and Taylor Sts.

Mount Baker Block -1890

architects: Whiteway and Schroeder

The year after most of the downtown buildings were constructed, Charles Eisenbeis erected his huge Mount Baker Block. It was originally planned to be a five-story, ninety-six room hotel costing $100,000. However, as work was about to begin in December 1889 another large "first-class" hotel was being planned. $50,000 was needed and Eisenbeis joined the promotion of the other hotel. In February 1890, he decided to construct a four-story business block with eight stores on the ground floor and sixty-nine offices above, complete with elevator. The projected cost was $80,000. Only the Kuhn Block, which was also to be a four-story, "first-class" hotel, at Polk and Water Streets, was to be more expensive at $100,000.

Tight money slowed construction during the summer of 1890. In the fall various businesses moved into the ground floor, but in November the bad news that the railroad would not be completed terminated construction of the building and the two top floors were left at the preliminary framing stage. The Kuhn Building suffered the same fate. Its top two floors were eventually torn off.

Though the **Leader** noted that, "The building will be of modern architecture and it will without doubt be one of the prettiest buildings in the city," by today's standards it is the most heavy-handed work of Whiteway and Schroeder. Both the Clarendon Hotel (Fowler-Caines Block) and the Sterming Block by the same firm, and dating from the previous year, show considerable architectural merit. One must assume that the desire for modernity—a pattern previously set in Seattle by architect Elmer Fisher—prompted Whiteway and Schroeder to compete in a style that they comprehended only superficially. The Richardsonian Romanesque was the most "modern" style in which to build at the time, but rather than having a satisfying

Mount Baker Block, Water and Tyler Sts.

massiveness, the Mount Baker Block appears as an inflated version of Fisher's Pioneer Building in Seattle but lacking Fisher's more delicate detailing and warmth of materials. Especially incomprehensible is the use of the large scaled arch on the fourth story at the corner. A bolder form than the tightly scaled arcade is introduced, only to be pointlessly nullified by heavy vertical divisions that seem to suggest that the arch needed shoring up.

The basement is of stone and there is some use of cast iron from the Port Townsend Foundry, especially at street level. The main fabric of the structure is cast stone and plastered brick—obdurate materials that defy a natural patination with age.

Despite its awkward design, the very bulk of the Mount Baker Block does have a stabilizing effect on the community. Approaching the center of the city, there is a psychological crescendo effect of increasingly large-scale structures which culminates at the corner of Water and Taylor. With the centrifugal energy that this core establishes, Port Townsend still maintains the cohesive, cosmopolitan quality of a city of importance.

Hastings Building-1889

architect: E.H. Fisher

Loren B. Hastings

Port Townsend's newspaper, the **Morning Leader**, observed in November 1889 that the Hastings Building, still under construction, was "conceded by all to be the most elegant building in the city." Noting that the cost was nearly $45,000, it went on to enumerate such progressive features as the two interior staircases, wainscotting of redwood, and the unusually large (96"x100") plate glass to be used on the first floor store fronts. "It has double floors throughout; the offices are all large and provided with every convenience and are arranged for either gas or electricity." Such amenities, not available in earlier Port Townsend office buildings, assured a full complement of tenants. The highly desirable corner location was occupied by a real estate office, which shared the ground floor with Enoch F. Plummer, "Cigars, Tobacco, Confectionary, and Smokers' Articles," Max Gerson Dry Goods, and Jarrett T. Lewis Co. Lewis advertised his groceries and staples regularly in the **Morning Leader** and the paper dutifully reported that, "His store in the new Hastings building is one of the most complete north of San Francisco." Lewis' advertisement in the 1890 Directory states that he has "Excellent teas, groceries, the finest Eastern canned goods, Sperry's noted flour, Key City flour, Hungarian process, Heinz renowned pickles, catsup, chow chow, etc."

The upper floors of the building were occupied by real estate offices, investment brokers, accountants, physicians, and an architect. These offices opened into an interior court with a skylight: an innovative plan used here for the first time in Port Townsend.

The foundation of the Hastings Estate Company, which built the structure, came from the fortune of Loren Brown Hastings, one of the original settlers of the town. In 1852 the federal government gave any

settler a donation claim of 320 acres (or double that for a married man). Plummer and Pettygrove filed claims close to the subsequent downtown. Hastings' claim continued along the waterfront, and included a great deal of the area he named Happy Valley. He farmed and operated a trading post and general store for several years and also dealt in real estate. He died in 1881 but members of his family continued to prosper in their own businesses. As the town expanded in the late 1880s, his farm became prime property for the burgeoning residential district. In 1890, Lucinda Hastings, his widow, had the highest tax assessment of any individual in the county, $118,490, on property worth much more than that. The entire Hastings family owned property which was assessed at $244,390.

Lucinda and six of her seven children built this building and formally established the Hastings Estate Company in 1890 with a capital stock of $600,000. (By comparison, most banks started with capital stocks of $50,000 to $75,000.)

Architect of the building was Elmer H. Fisher of Seattle. Fisher emigrated from Scotland at the age of seventeen. He studied architecture in Massachusetts and drifted west via Minnesota, Colorado, and Victoria, B.C., arriving in Seattle in 1888. The great Seattle fire of 1889 gave him the opportunity to make a major impact on Puget Sound architecture and he designed and supervised the construction of more than fifty buildings in the two-year period that followed. Henry Yesler's Pioneer Building in Seattle is perhaps his best known surviving work, though the Austin A. Bell building on First near Battery and the Schwabacher Building on First south of Yesler are also prominent among Seattle's historic structures.

The influence of H.H. Richardson, predictable in any architect trained in New England in the late nineteenth century, is obvious in Fisher's work, though more so in Seattle's Pioneer Building than in any of Fisher's three known Port Townsend buildings. In the Hastings Building a conservative Romanesque style is the most obvious design motif and the bay windows projecting from the second and third stories give the structure a massive undulating form. Bays are useful devices in commercial buildings; they increase the potential window area in the individual offices as well as gain useful interior space. Fisher's choice of the Romanesque over other fashionable eclectic forms (Tudor, Gothic, Italianate, for example) necessarily gives his bay treatment greater bulk and visual weight than one customarily sees. Whereas Richardson used the Romanesque partly because it demanded less decorative accessories than other Victorian sub-styles and allowed wall surfaces to stand unadorned, Fisher is more typically Victorian in his love of decoration. His embellishment of surface is almost total. (The corner tower was originally adorned with a turret

Hastings Bldg. interior from third floor.

roof and flagpole and the truncated mansard roof had a cresting of decorative iron.) Richardson also tended to minimize the visual division between stories for the sake of overall unity. But Fisher, in his provincial interpretation, used a strong definition of horizontals at each floor level and articulated the window entablatures to the point that each opening in the facade is seen as a separate entity.

By the time construction began on the Hastings Building, Port Townsend was less dependent upon building materials brought in by ship. The cast iron columns at street level, seen to particular advantage flanking the handsome west entry, were cast by the Port Townsend Foundry which had been established in 1883. Of all the materials used in construction, only the ceilings of the stores, patented embossed iron that imitated decorative plaster and was currently thought to be "fireproof," is recorded as being imported, and these were from Northrup Company in Pittsburgh.

The Hastings Building was built during Port Townsend's boom period when optimism was high. In 1889 it was the most expensive construction in the city, but it held this distinction scarcely a year.

Hastings Bldg. exterior detail.

Hastings Bldg. first floor detail.

Hastings Bldg. west door.

61

N.D. Hill Building - 1889

architect: E.H. Fisher

N.D. Hill

In 1888 Nathanial Davis Hill retired at the age of sixty-five and turned over the N.D. Hill and Sons Drug Co. to his sons Daniel and Howard. The following year, presumably with his sons, he undertook an ambitious development of his corner lot and construction began on one of Port Townsend's major buildings.

Hill was from Pennsylvania and had been trained in medicine. He arrived at Whidbey Island in 1852 and took the customary 320-acre land claim and became Indian Agent. In 1857 he returned east to marry his fiancee of six years, Sallie Haddock. They returned to the west and survived a Pacific storm so violent that Mrs. Hill's household possessions had to be jettisoned. This, plus the news on arrival at Whidbey Island that Colonel Ebey had been beheaded by raiding Indians the week before, was hardly the sort of adventure and romance that eastern periodicals might have led the new bride to expect.

The Hills moved to Port Townsend in 1868 and Mr. Hill was active in a variety of businesses in addition to his drugstore. His brother, Robert, who had joined him in the 1850s, was also involved in numerous profitable Puget Sound enterprises and was one of the founders of the First National Bank. Before Hill bought this site in 1868 there had been a small brick building on the same location which was built as the custom house but later became a drug store operated by Dr. P.M. O'Brien. The new three-story building with the drugstore occupying the choice corner position provided also for Lawrence Portman's Crockery and Glassware at the street level and for upstairs offices and apartments. Hill listed himself at this location in the 1890 Directory: "Nathaniel D. Hill, Capitalist".

Seattle architect Elmer H. Fisher had another building under construction in Port Townsend at this time (see Hastings Building).

N.D. Hill Building, Water and Quincy Sts.

Bar in N.D. Hill Bldg.

N.D. Hill Building interior from third floor.

Either because of a less generous budget or a desire not to become stereotyped he projects a somewhat different image in the Hill Building. Though similar in scale and utilizing a skylighted central court as in the Hastings Building, here we see a more self-contained mass and less dependence upon cast iron from the Port Townsend Foundry. Though the stylish drugstore entrance on the diagonal is framed by columns with cast iron bases, the strip pilasters that extend through the three stories and divide the facades into bays are of brick. This economy in materials, plus elimination of the projecting bays so prominent in the Hastings Building, allowed the construction cost to be about $25,000 (vs. $45,000 for the Hastings Building). The Hill Building design is very reminiscent of some of Fisher's Seattle work. The Bay Building at First and University uses the same pattern of fenestration with square-headed window entablatures on the lower floors and a conservatively small-scale arcade of Romanesque arches on the top story. It also has strip pilasters for the vertical divisions and a pronounced belt course forming the horizontal divisions. The bracketed metalwork cornice with an arched pediment centered in each of the vertical bays is particularly fine in the Hill Building. Though bold cornices appear also in Fisher's Bay and Pioneer Buildings it is only in the latter that the architect uses the Richardsonian device of attempting to group individual windows into units enclosed by a larger scaled arch. Fisher's windows are almost always precisely articulated and seen as separate entities. The brickwork and metalcraft are fine examples of late nineteenth century craftmanship and though not stylistically progressive, the building used the flexible interior courtyard plan and incorporated one of Port Townsend's first elevators.

The Victorian bar in the Town Tavern, almost a piece of architecture in its own right, was moved to the building from another location. It seems to have been a fixture in Port Townsend since the late nineteenth century. Seemingly all square grand pianos and bars are reputed to have "come around the Horn" including this and a similar one at Friday Harbor. Prior to the advent of the railroad all manufactured goods from the east were of necessity brought around the Horn or laboriously hauled across the portage at Panama. This bar might equally well have come by ship or railroad.

Detail of bar in N.D. Hill Building

Detail of bar in N.D. Hill Building

James & Hastings Building -1889 architects: Fisher and Clark

On property owned jointly by Francis W. James and Lucinda Hastings, the James & Hastings building, completed in early 1889 for $24,000, was occupied before many of the other large buildings. There were offices and apartments upstairs; Smith, Ellis, and Co., Dry Goods, on the ground floor at the corner entrance, and L.B. Hastings and Co. in the other space on the ground floor. Smith, Ellis, and Co.'s advertisement in the October 3, 1890 **Morning Leader** gives an indication of their wares, "New Goods! New Goods! New Goods! Elegant Line of Ladies' Cloth, Silks, Plushes, Velvets, and French Flannels; Children's and Youths' Clothing, Furnishing Goods, Shoes &c., &c. The Famous I.C. Corsets and Antoinette Gloves". L.B. Hastings, Lucinda and Loren's son, was operating a rapidly growing store in addition to his other activities as president of the Commercial Wharf and his steamboat line. He carried a large and diversified stock, including stoves and ranges (800 in stock), tools, plumbing goods, brass goods, cutlery, tinware (a tinshop was in the rear) and contracted plumbing and gas fitting, heating and steamboat work.

The stolidly conservative design of the James & Hastings Building by Seattle architects Fisher and Clark seems to visually express the almost universal Victorian conviction that a solid brick building at a good location was the safest possible investment. The three very distinct "layers" of the building are intricately fenestrated with small-scale openings that emphasize the weight of the masonry. With sufficient ornament, reaching a crescendo at the elaborate sheet metal cornice, it epitomizes middle class merchant taste. Unlike the Capt. Tibbals Block, built concurrently and in an "open" design, the

James and Hastings Building, Water and Tyler Sts.

architect's conception in the James & Hastings Building seems entirely reclusive. Interesting in its details, the interlocking window entablatures of cast stone are curious and unusual. Though somewhat disruptive of the handsome brick masonry, the vertical continuity of the pilasters carries through from ground floor to cornice and lends a satisfying authority.

James and Hastings Building

Terry Building-1890

Fred M. Terry was listed at various times as a dairyman, farmer, contractor, and superintendent of the Port Townsend Electric Street Railway, Power and Light Company. He brought the first locomotive engine to the Olympic Peninsula, **"Sadie"**, used for grading streets. His building was used for a printing shop and apartments.

Following completion of the $8,000 building, six liens were filed against it: Quimper Manufacturing (sash, doors and blinds), Tacoma Lumber, Tacoma Cornice Works, George W. Downs (lumber), L.B. Hastings and Co. (hardware, stoves, plumbing and gasfitting), and Kreher and Desmond (painters). Though this list must have been an embarrassment for Terry and his partners, it provides interesting documentation of the Terry Building unmatched by any other construction in Port Townsend.

Victorian architecture is often criticized as being an "art of assemblage" and the extensive list of suppliers, the wide variety of materials (masonry, wood, cast iron, and sheet metal), and the "pieced-together-look" of the building would seem to partially justify such criticism. However, the Terry Building, having never been remodelled on the first floor, as is so often the case with older buildings, is a most interesting total survivor.

The simple and effective pedimented cornice detail is repeated on the two projecting bays. The recessed doorways, flanked by cast iron from the Port Townsend Foundry, give weather protection to the wooden doors as well as an interesting complexity of receding and projecting planes in the building's facade. Though the bays and masonry wall above seem somewhat too massive for the structure at street level and though it was seemingly not designed by a professional architect, as a vernacular structure, it is a unique and interesting example.

Terry Building, Washington St.

Siebenbaum Building - 1903

John Siebenbaum, a native of Germany, came to Port Townsend in the mid-1880s and opened the Bavaria Beer Hall, and later the Milwaukee Saloon in Charles Eisenbeis' second building (now the Puget Power office). He developed a prosperous wholesale and retail liquor business and became proprietor of the Delmonico, "one of the best patronized and appointed bars to be found." The **Morning Leader** commented, "At the Delmonico will be found good cheer and congenial company always, the best of goods at right prices, and honorable treatment." While proprietor of the Delmonico, Siebenbaum constructed this building in the same block as his bar. It was leased to two other long-time residents of the town, Joseph Steiner, who operated his cigar store on the ground floor, and Dr. O'Rear, a dentist on the second floor. In addition, the building was "cosily fitted up in excellent apartments."

Though built in the early twentieth century at a time when Port Townsend's economy had slumped to its nadir, the Siebenbaum Building displays no technical or stylistic advancement from its Victorian predecessors. The curiously proportioned gable that rises from the bracketed cornice is an indecisive shape hovering between Gothic and classic and the overscaled bays would seem to indicate that the building was a vernacular amalgamation of ideas gleaned from earlier Port Townsend facades, and particularly indebted to the 1889 Sterming Block.

Siebenbaum Building, Water St.

City Hall - 1891

architects: Batwell & Patrick

The optimistic outlook over Port Townsend's future growth and prosperity had led both the County and Federal governments to invest in impressive architectural projects. Not to be outdone, Port Townsend citizens in 1891 voted overwhelmingly to build a City Hall which was to cost $30,000. Though the railroad had already gone into receivership and economic stagnation that was to follow had already commenced, at the time this was viewed as but a temporary setback. Instead of the quick amortization of the debt that might have been expected, it stretched out for fifty years. Ironically, by the time it was paid off, wind damage had necessitated the removal of the roof and tower—leaving the building somewhat truncated in appearance.

The sedate architecture, by local architects Batwell and Patrick, employs sandstone for the foundation, sills, lintels and capitals. The last are richly and imaginatively carved in a loosely interpreted Romanesque design. Though local brick is the dominant structural material for walls and pilasters, its sober utilization in traditional forms makes the vigorously flamboyant art nouveau motif of the embossed sheet metal cornice all the more unexpected and impressive.

In addition to being the City Hall, the building now houses the Jefferson County Historical Museum in what had been the fire hall and police court rooms.

City Hall, Water and Madison Sts.

City Hall with third floor.

City Council Chambers.

Stone carving at entrance to City Hall.

City Hall capital with bird above first floor.

Jefferson County Courthouse - 1892

architect: Willis A. Ritchie

With business and property values soaring, and prosperity
seemingly ensured, the citizens of Jefferson County voted in 1889 to
build a new courthouse. It would be much more splendid than the
Fowler building, which had served that function for many years. The
size of the bond issue was restricted by law to 1½ percent of the total
assessed valuation of property in the county, and the initial plan for a
$100,000 building would have been too expensive. But when the 1890
assessment was recorded the following summer, the property values
were much higher and the county could go ahead with the plan. The
County Commissioners were to judge the eight plans submitted in
competition. These plans were supposedly to remain anonymous
during the judging but the June 27 and June 28, 1890 **Morning Leaders**,
strongly advocating the plan of a 26-year-old Seattle architect, W.A.
Ritchie, published the identity of the various contestants prior to the
final decision and outrageously praised Ritchie's plan as "by far the
most handsome and imposing structure...". Ritchie's entry of "an
absolutely fireproof" plan met the commissioners' standards of
grandeur and price and he was given the commission.

The original plan, as described in the July 2, 1890 **Morning
Leader**, was for a $100,000 Romanesque building 75 x 140 feet, with a
stone basement on the ground floor and native pressed brick, stone,
terra cotta, and pressed metal trimmings above. The tower was 20 feet
square and 140 feet high with an observatory at 80 feet, and a clock
with 10-foot faces at the top. The basement had a fuel room and boiler
room with two large boilers, 10 jails 6'6" x 8'6" to hold 4 people each,
a dungeon 7' x 9' and a "light" cell for insane people. There were two
courtrooms on the second floor, 40' x 60' and 27' x 36', with ceilings 18
and 20 feet high. Steel beams and hollow tile fire proof floor arches

Jefferson County Courthouse, west facade

were used throughout. No wood was used except for the roof trusses over the large courtroom, rafters, tower floors above the attic, and the tower roof. The attic rooms had wire lath on the underside of the rafters and a plaster ceiling with tin shingles on the roof "so that no fire could possibly reach the rafters to burn them."

Contractor John A. Rigby employed fifty-five men and had a monthly payroll of $4,500 - $5,000. He employed eleven stonecutters at $4.50 for an eight-hour day, twelve brickmasons at $4.00 a day, and several laborers at $2.00 to $2.50 a day. With a few changes (the four million bricks came from St. Louis, and the tower is 124'4" high), the building was completed as planned in 1892, at a total cost, including jail and furnishings, of more than $150,000.

The bell and clock were built to order by the E. Howard Watch and Clock Co. of Boston and installed in 1892 for $3,497. When the courthouse was wired for electricity in 1912, the clock faces were illuminated and an electric motor was installed to wind the weights and counterbalances, a job which reportedly had taken two men half a day to accomplish before.

Willis A. Ritchie, originally from Ohio, was largely a self-trained architect, who at the age of twenty-three already had an impressive list of accomplishments including schools, banks and two county courthouses in Kansas. He had come to Seattle immediately after the 1889 fire and had been given the contract for the King County Court-house and the Whatcom County Courthouse. (Later he would also design courthouses for Clark County in Vancouver, Thurston County in Olympia, and Spokane County as well as Jefferson County.)

In Betty McDonald's book, **The Egg and I**, she described Port Townsend, "The Town", and summarized: "She wore her massive courthouse like an enormous brooch on a delicate bosom..." Massive indeed is the courthouse, but in a satisfying nineteenth century monumental way. One might criticize Ritchie's work as being too facile, too undisciplined. But for all its faults the architecture of the Jefferson County Courthouse is rewarding for the skilled manner in which the bulky massiveness of stone is juxtaposed against the smooth, flat areas of brick and rewarding as well for the high quality sculptured details in random and unpredictable locations.

Richardson himself had no rivals in his ability to handle the Romanesque forms that he popularized, but many architects handled the mode less skillfully than Ritchie and the great arched entry dominating the west facade is a powerful and impressive feature. Ironically, it is in the rear of the building where the more fashionable and sometimes too chaotic forms yield to the functional and unadorned parts of the building such as the smokestack, where Ritchie comes the nearest to capturing the spirit of his famous predecessor who established the roots of modern architecture.

Jefferson County Courthouse, north side, Inset shows east side clock face.

Jefferson County Courthouse, clock mechanism

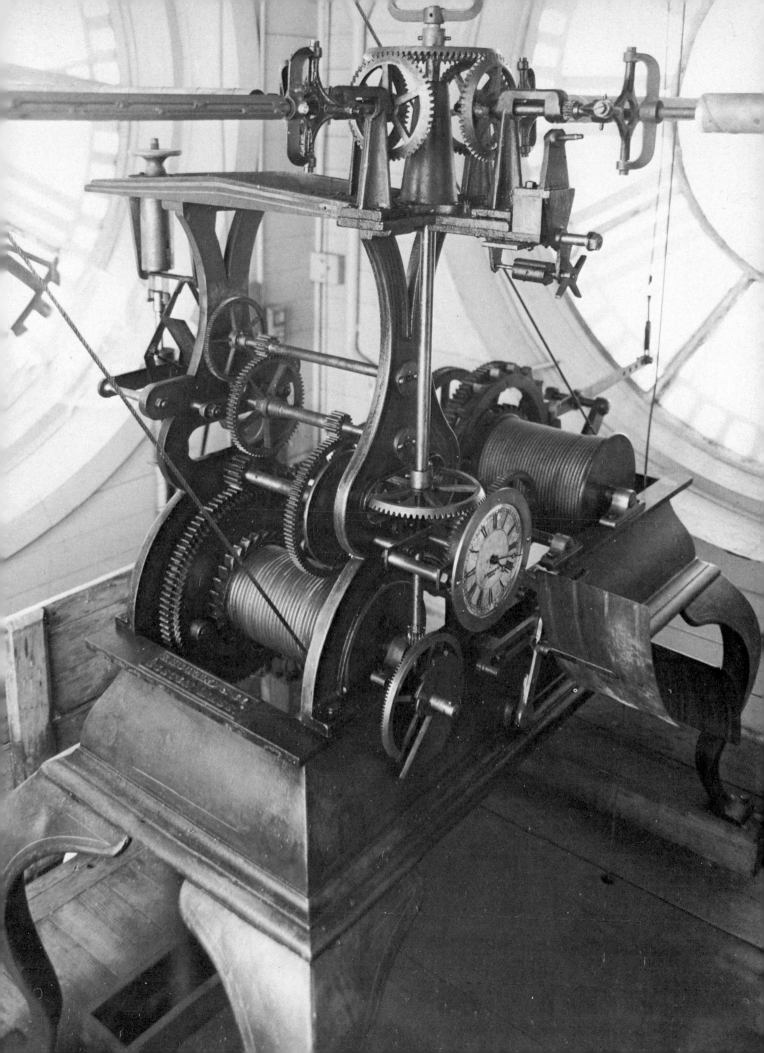

West side entrance to courthouse.

Custom House and Post Office - 1893

The Custom House was the most important factor in Port Townsend's early economy. Since the town was the port of entry for the Puget Sound, every ship that entered or left had to register there. Crews were paid off there, and most sailors stayed and spent their wages until they signed on for another voyage. The ships bought their supplies from Port Townsend stores. In the late 1880 s, shipping added $4,000,000 annually to the economy of Port Townsend, which was second only to New York in total tonnage registered by customs.

For many years the customs work had been done in wooden buildings by the docks. In March, 1885, Congress appropriated $70,000 for the purpose of building a new custom house. After a series of expansions and changes of plans, a total of $240,000 was appropriated. The first contract was awarded in 1887, and work continued sporadically from that time. In April, 1889, when only the foundation had been completed, Judge John N. Scott, President Harrison's brother-in-law, was appointed to superintend the project. Work continued slowly, and on March 1, 1893, the building was completed at a cost of $241,822.81, making it by far the most expensive building in town. Although the economy had been suffering for nearly three years, several ships still registered in Port Townsend, since the town was still the headquarters for the customs district.

The previous design for the Custom House was more academic in concept—an Italianate building with an impressive tower based on the design of the Mausoleum at Halicarnassus, one of the Seven Wonders of the World. In a later design a six-story tower was planned at the right of the south entrance to add "majesty" and to provide a good view of the incoming ships. To save money, however, only three stories were actually built. The faces of local Indians were carved into

Custom House and Post Office, Washington and Harrison Sts.

the capitals of the columns on either side of the south entrance. The settlers' names for these Indians were "the Duke of York, Queen Victoria, King George, and Jenny Lind." The wind blew so fiercely during the winter that the south entry was blocked off and the main access is now from the east side. Two thirds of the main floor has always served as the post office.

Though the **Morning Leader** January 1, 1892 described the Custom House, at that time nearing completion, as "a landmark to be pointed out to strangers as a thing of beauty and joy forever," this massive and somber structure today is more likely to generate awe than exhilaration. Federal architecture in the nineteenth century was monumental and conservative. Prior to the Civil War, in an age of optimism and independence, the Greek Revival forms that were employed were an American invention. The disillusionment of the decades following the war were reflected in eclectic architectural forms more directly dependent upon European prototypes, almost as though a national inferiority complex dictated that American styles were provincial and should give way to those of older cultures. The architect's intention in this design was patently to create an impressive monumental structure alleviated by picturesque qualities borrowed from European Romanesque sources. H.H. Richardson, in his designs for governmental and academic buildings, also used Romanesque forms but with a different purpose: one of simplification. Consequently, in Richardsonian Romanesque one seldom sees such a random scattering of window openings or such variety of shapes and proportions in the fenestration. Especially, had the tower been completed (as it is pictured in **Port Townsend Illustrated**), it would have more nearly approximated a German Rhineland fortification than Richardson's archetypal buildings in New England and the Middle Atlantic states. The handsome stonework is actually a veneer over brick, making the walls 28" thick. The interior spaces that originally reinforced the monumentality of the exterior have been remodelled and some ceilings lowered but the rich detailing of the iron newel post and wrought iron railing on the stair suggest how the second story courtroom once appeared.

Stairway in Custom House and Post Office

Custom House and Post Office detail showing Chetzemoka ("Duke of York") and Queen Victoria

Port Townsend Steel, Wire, and Nail Co. -1892

After the Port Townsend and Southern Railroad went into receivership, part of the property was sold to Eastern capitalists to be used as a nail factory (mass produced wire nails were rapidly displacing the previously expensive handcrafted "square" nails at this time). Many local businessmen were encouraged by the project after the disappointment of the railroad failure, and invested heavily in it. The factory, built on pilings in 1892, was filled with expensive machinery. It employed 200 men, but closed after a few years, and the machinery was moved to Everett.

About fifteen years after that, Edgar Sims, who later became an influential state senator, opened a salmon cannery in the building as an expansion of his prosperous fishing business. It also closed after a few years.

To contemporary architects who find the sentimental and romantic aspects of Victorian architecture cloying and uninspired, industrial architecture of the period provides the greatest interest. Such structures as these were rarely designed by either architects or engineers but they satisfy that twentieth century cliche, "Form follows function", that has taken on such mystical significance. Actually, these industrial buildings have a positive aesthetic quality to the twentieth century observer that was never intended. They merely provided the maximum amount of enclosed space by the most economic means of construction. The truss construction, clerestory lighting, and taut sheathing are only incidentally and accidentally seen as objects of beauty "in the eyes of the beholder."

Port Townsend Steel, Wire, and Nail Company, Washington and Benedict Sts.

Inset from Company stationary letterhead

Churches

St. Paul's Episcopal Church-1865

St. Paul's was completed for about $2,000 in 1865 by A. Horace Tucker, an early builder, under the direction of Rev. Peter E. Hyland. At the time, Port Townsend's population was approximately 300. The original site had been donated by Loren B. Hastings, close to the spot where the Lucinda Hastings house was built several years later. The church was moved by horse and windlass to its present location in 1883. The Rectory was built in 1888 in a compatible style. The move damaged the structure to the extent that iron tie-rods, still to be seen in the interior, had to be placed between the opposite walls.

Captain J.W. Selden, of the revenue cutter **Wyanda**, was navigating through the fog by dead reckoning when he heard a school bell which Rev. Hyland used to summon his parishioners. Turning his ship, he avoided running onto the rocks and, in appreciation, he brought the present bell on his next trip to Port Townsend and gave it to the church on the condition that it be rung on foggy days. Years later, the steamship **Liza Anderson** was lost in the fog on its run from Victoria to Seattle, but the bell guided her to safety. Ira Sankey, the evangelist, was a passenger on the ship, and the incident inspired him to write **The Harbor Bell**, a hymn that became widely popular.

The main chancel was changed in 1896, and a new altar built to accommodate the main window, which was donated by Ann van Bokkelen Starrett in memory of her brother, John A. van Bokkelen, who died in the Victoria bridge disaster that year. The stained glass windows on the sides are a recent addition.

The Gothic Revival style had been popularized in the United States by Andrew Jackson Downing. Downing's sudden ascendency in the 1840s as a national arbiter of taste was largely responsible for the

St. Paul's Episcopal Church, Jefferson and Tyler Sts.

waning of classical motifs prior to the Civil War. The pattern books of the time that guided builders and carpenters had, by the 1860s, taken up an enthusiastic advocacy of the Gothic style. St. Paul's was undoubtedly a pattern book conception and the elegance of its proportions and consistency in styling, inside and out, was hardly accidental. Unlike the popular conceptions of what "Victorian Architecture" implies, this Victorian church is almost completely devoid of ornament and its effectiveness depends almost completely on the repetition of vertical proportions, angular relationships of form and structure, and subtle refinements of execution. Perhaps the most unusual and effective subtlety is the use of a bold exterior grid applied to the walls that divides the clapboard sheathing into panels. Though not completely structural—as it appears at first glance—this grid visually gives weight and mass to walls that otherwise would be thin and unarticulated. This quite innovative means of giving monumentality to a wooden structure of modest scale is surprisingly effective and satisfying.

Interior of St. Paul's

First United Presbyterian Church - 1890

architects - Whiteway and Schroeder

The only congregation which felt that it was necessary to build a larger church during the boom was the Presbyterians. Under the direction of Rev. Carnahan, the congregation of fewer than 100 built a $16,000 church which had a capacity of 600. Regretfully they tore down a charming stone church which had been dedicated on this site twelve years before, and used the stone as the foundation of their new wooden church, which was dedicated March 16, 1890.

Designed by local architects, Whiteway and Schroeder, it was "thoroughly modern", having a furnace, combination gas and electrical fixtures, and full carpeting on the floor. George Chapman, "one of the best fresco artists in the United States" according to the **Morning Leader**, painted the ceiling and walls of the sanctuary, but these were eventually damaged by moisture, and were plastered over.

The tracker action organ was made by Whalley and Genung of Oakland, California for $2,500. It has 692 pipes ranging in length from two inches to sixteen feet. The front is eastern walnut, and the pipes were painted, perhaps also by Chapman, in colors which were harmonious with the interior decoration.

Though the January 1, 1890 **Morning Leader** reports that the "magnificent" building nearing completion "is purely Gothic", one might better describe the style as a four-square version of Queen Anne with Gothic and Stick Style motifs. The interesting variety of textures and materials used in the building are a typical feature of this transitional decade in American architecture, but Whiteway and Schroeder have not so skillfully endowed their structure with any continuity of form or decoration as did the anonymous designer of the nearby St. Paul's Episcopal church. Essentially the thin, two-dimensional quality of the decoration is the predominent feature (hardly any of the applied

First United Presbyterian Church, Franklin and Polk Sts.

ornament is in sufficient relief to cast shadows or create highlights). In consequence the geometry of the structure's complex volumes is predominent over the linear decorative scheme. The bell tower, though not uninteresting in design, is awkwardly related to the roof forms and inexplicably introduces a motif of segmental arched openings instead of picking up either the lancet Gothic forms or semi-circular openings of the lower tower. The striking pyramidal tower roof, though effective at a distance, at close range tends to impose a near-insuperable weight on the delicately detailed understructure.

Church architecture often communicates both secular and spiritual attitudes and values of the congregation and one might deduce from this church that the Port Townsend Presbyterians in 1890 were prosperous, ambitious, and practical. The lofty interior space, with pews arranged in concentric circles, places strong emphasis on the pulpit—a particularly favored Presbyterian plan in this age of notable preachers.

Whalley and Genung Organ in First United Presbyterian Church.

Residences

Capt. Tibbals house
- c. 1860

Capt. Henry L. Tibbals established himself as one of Port Townsend's more colorful people during his long life there. Before his arrival in 1853, he had spent most of his life on the sea. At ten, he became a cabin boy, and by twenty he was a master sailor. In his youth, he experimented with diving bells to reclaim sunken treasure. He became a pilot of the revenue cutter **Jeff Davis**, but retired in 1858 to open the second hotel in Port Townsend, the Pioneer, which later became the Cosmopolitan. This proved to be very lucrative during the Fraser River goldrush, and he was able to build this house shortly thereafter. He also built the Union wharf at the foot of Taylor Street with Loren B. Hastings and H.H. Hibbard. He was manager of the wharf and agent for the Pacific Steamboat Company, which offered direct service between Port Townsend and San Francisco. He served in a variety of public offices, including territorial legislator, sheriff, county commissioner, city council, and postmaster.

He was fond of horses and was often seen at public celebrations parading around and officiating. On one occasion, he rode his horse into a saloon and ordered drinks for everyone. He started a one-mile racetrack in 1889 which he claimed would be "one of the fastest in the world."

Tibbals' later years were considerably less happy. He divorced his wife, Caroline, in 1887 to marry another woman. The sympathy of the townspeople was with Caroline, and Tibbals' new wife, Josephine, apparently commanded no respect at all. Tibbals built his bride a $10,000 house on the outskirts of town. She later deserted him, but returned with her father and brother-in-law, and, according to the June 19, 1892 **Leader**, "assaulted, choked, and beat (Tibbals) in the most unmerciful manner, to the great danger of his life and loss of

Capt. H.L. Tibbals house

health," This was too much for the captain, then in his sixties, and he divorced Josephine, too. Although his son was very successful, Tibbals spent his last years in poverty, and died penniless in 1920.

Of all the surviving early Port Townsend houses, the Tibbals and Tucker houses alone are in the classic Greek Revival style. Though the Fowler and Rothschild houses were built in the same decade, they are based on earlier New England architecture of the Federal period and have a thinness in the articulation of porch details and corner trim not seen here. The original house seems to have been a simple rectangle with a flat-roofed portico supported by square full-bodied doric columns, extending out from the gable end. The low-pitched roof, wide fascia board, and serene proportions are elemental attributes in that period of vigor and restraint that characterized American architecture in the pre-Civil War period. It would appear that in the 1870s the large wing was extended to the left of the main house. Later, another column was added to the portico so that it would cover a second door leading into the wing. The architecture of the addition followed the restraint of the original structure in proportion and detailing—even to repeating the generous scale of the window lights— and only in the Victorian panelled door is there a clue to its later date. At some time after the 1870s the bay window was added to the north.

Unlike most houses of the period which used the utilitarian and economic balloon frame construction invented in America in the 1830s, the main body of the Tibbals house employs the older mode of box construction, using 2x16s butted vertically and extending from basement to attic.

Though not competing for attention with the flamboyant architecture of later decades when Port Townsend had reached an apogee of exuberance and expectation, the Tibbals house is as fine and forthright an example of pioneer architecture as any surviving in Washington.

E.S. Fowler house
– c. 1860

Capt. Enoch S. Fowler arrived shortly after the first settlers and made Port Townsend his home in 1852. Early in 1854 he purchased the schooner **R.B. Potter** and chartered it to Governor Stevens as a mail and dispatch boat. After its release from territorial service, he operated it as the first regular mail packet on the route between Olympia, Seattle, Port Townsend, and Victoria. Retiring from the sea in 1857, he built the first dock in Port Townsend, held several public offices, dealt in real estate, and built the first two-story stone building in town in 1874. He died two years later. Although this house was probably built by A.A. Plummer or F.W. Pettygrove, who previously owned the property, Fowler is the first known occupant, having bought the house in 1864. It and the Capt. Tibbals' house are the oldest surviving residences in town.

The style of the house is based on prototypes of the early settlers' homes in New England. Conservative Federal architecture, rectangular in plan and self-contained under a simple gable roof (the summer kitchen to the rear was probably a later addition), it originally would have had a rectangular flat-roofed and balustraded porch extending along the south facade as in the Rothschild house. The clapboard walls and shuttered windows were typical of middle class dwellings when the United States was a Republic and the population was dispersed in rural areas and seacoast villages. Such houses, solid in construction and sensible in plan (and in this instance endowed with ample window glass) would seldom survive unaltered into the later Victorian era when applied decorative details became a necessary mark of prosperity and taste.

Fowler house, Polk and Jefferson Sts.

D.C.H. Rothschild house -1868

Rothschild was a Bavarian who was only related to the banking family, "Just enough to get the name, not the money." He opened the Kentucky store on Water Street in 1858. "The Baron," as he was called, was an astute and popular businessman in the community for many years. In 1881 he and his sons sold the mercantile business and opened a shipping and commission business.

For ten years he lived over the Kentucky store, then in 1868 he had this house built by A.H. Tucker, a contractor who referred to it as the "Rothschild Mansion". The house stayed in the Rothschild family. Emilie, the youngest daughter and a spinster, lived there for many years and maintained the house and furnishings much as her parents had left them. It was given to the city in 1959 by a surviving son and later was acquired by the Washington State Parks and Recreation Commission for use as a museum.

Houses such as the Rothschilds' would have been comparatively common on the west coast in the decades of the 1850s and 1860s. Based on New England precedents, they reinterpreted the classic revival forms of the Colonial and Federal period and were simple in construction and unassertive in form. Few have survived in their original condition for the mere fact that in the following decades of greater architectural pretension, their unassuming forms and simple interior volumes were either elaborated or "improved" by the addition of applied ornament, or expanded as the need for space dictated. Such architectural puritanism has a far different appeal than the High Victorian style that characterizes most of Port Townsend's architecture and the crisply geometric house—no more than a decorated box—stands serenely apart from its neighbors.

Rothschild house, Taylor and Jefferson Sts.

A.H. Tucker house -1867

A. Horace Tucker brought his carpentry skills and a set of building plans to Port Townsend in 1862. He joined his father who had left their Portsmouth, New Hampshire home several years before in search of California gold. Tucker constructed many of Port Townsend's early buildings, including the Rothschild house and St. Paul's church. That church's first wedding was Tucker's marriage to Jane Caines in 1867. In that year he built this house, which he occupied until his death in 1938 at the age of 99.

In addition to being a house builder, he was also a coffin maker, mayor, and holder of a variety of other public offices. Joining the building boom in the 1880s, he opened a brickyard at Point Wilson, and erected a $25,000 (Whiteway and Schroeder designed) three-story brick building at Water and Adams Streets, which has since been demolished.

Though much changed from its original appearance due to the remodelling of the 1890s, the Tucker house still gives evidence of its Greek Revival origins: the substantial doric pilasters at the corners, the pedimented front with its wide fascia, and the classic proportions of the gable. Port Townsend's obsession with bay windows in this instance transforms what had been a "temple" into an impressive "cottage". The original intention in the design was to obliterate any exterior indication of a second floor in order to emphasize its simplicity and unity. The later additions establish an intermediate horizontal division awkwardly uncoordinated with the impressive pilasters.

A. Horace Tucker house

Capt. James McIntyre house - c. 1871

Capt. McIntyre, a Scot, married Sophie Pettygrove, daughter of one of Port Townsend's founders, November 17, 1865. Six years later they bought this property from her father, adjacent to his house. Within a few years they built the first section of the house, consisting of a rectangular plan with a kitchen wing at the rear. The side section and the bays were added later.

Capt. McIntyre was in charge of several boats over the years. He spent most of his life on the sea. In 1902 his steamer **Bristol** struck a rock on the Alaskan coast, and the 70-year-old captain went down with his ship.

The relatively early date of this house is quite effectively disguised by the Victorian additions that appear to date from the 1880s. However the low pitch of the roof and broad proportions of the gable end of the house, with its emphatically scaled fascia board, indicate a house that was designed and built prior to the late Victorian stylistic preference for vertical proportions. In this instance the alliance of styles is successfully integrated and the classic proportions and simple gable roof seem an appropriate and sobering framework on which the bracketed window entablatures, projecting bays, and delicately ornamented porch have been superimposed. A fashionable house of the 1880 period would have been set on a higher foundation with steps leading to the front porch, but the remodelling could not alter the existing floor level and the intimacy in the relationship of the earlier house to its site survives as an unexpected attribute.

Capt. James MacIntyre house, Lawrence and Van Buren Sts.

John Fuge house
- c. 1879

In 1879, John E. Fuge, a Welsh ship's carpenter, bought three blocks of view property along the bluff in what was then the outskirts of town. He built a series of houses, for the use of family and for rental, and continued to own most of the lots well into the twentieth century. This house, the largest, was for his own use.

Port Townsend has a wealth of variations on the bracketed bay. Often they were added to earlier houses to update an outmoded style (for example, Tucker and McIntyre houses) and they occasionally survive into the 1890s and are seen in a Queen Anne context. However, here we see a fine example contemporary with the architecture of the house. The low hipped roof, wide bracketed cornice, and the vertical proportions of this self-contained house are all typical of the Italianate Villa style but the consistency and restraint in the use of decoration and the unusually broad five window bays make this house a particularly pleasing example. Interior details, typical of the period, have survived as remarkably intact as the exterior—including wood graining on doors and trim, original wallpaper in entry hall and parlor, and staircase carpet. A less typical feature is a built-in zinc bathtub in the kitchen.

Fuge house, Washington St.

Henry Landes house -1882

Col. Henry Landes

"Colonel Landes is of commanding presence, over six feet in height, and weighs 220 pounds." So reported the **Morning Leader** on November 8, 1889. Landes was born in Germany, but emigrated to Kentucky when he was three. He lived there until, as the same article puts it, "Breaking away from the restraints of school in the latter part of 1861, he enlisted in a Kentucky Union regiment." After the war, he headed west, spending time in the British Columbia gold fields and Neah Bay before moving to Port Townsend in 1876.

In addition to establishing the First National Bank, Henry Landes affected the community in several other capacities. He was city treasurer, city councilman, director and treasurer of the Port Townsend Southern Railroad, member of the Big Five real estate syndicate, appointee to various government committees and military positions, and an effective state senator representing three counties.

The house has had several additions. The main right-hand section was originally a part of a large house that was built sometime between 1871 and 1876 by Susan B. Dennison and later sold to Solomon Katz and resold to Susan Dennison. In 1882, Landes moved it to a more central location on the lot and added the left-hand section. He remodelled again in 1887, adding a bay, and a cellar and one room to the back. Since then, extensive additions were made in the rear, but the front appears today much as it did after 1887, with the exception that the porch was extended to include the front bay.

It was one of the attributes of the Queen Anne style that it could be applied so casually to structures that were considered old-fashioned or un-stylish. Shingle surfaces could be applied to break up areas of

Henry Landes house, Polk and Franklin Sts.

clapboard. Decoration could be nailed onto bargeboards or fitted into gables and porches, and bays could be extended outward and upward—all without changing the basic structure of the original building. The Landes house quite effectively disguises the severity of the original 1870s rectangular structure and the hybrid nature of the additions which were added in the 1880s.

Though ideally the roof forms of Queen Anne architecture would have been more romantic and broken, at least chimney forms could be elaborated and dramatized. Exemplifying the love of angular or curvilinear forms, the newer gabled section to the left with its diagonal corners is more typical of architecture in the final decade of the century, yet the very contrast and tension between the unmatching gables was itself deemed a virtue. The unifying effect of the broad porch, which ties the disparate forms into a surprising harmony, seems to have been calculated as both an aesthetic and functional amenity.

Alexander's Castle
– c. 1883

The Reverend J.B. Alexander, English by birth (he later served as English consul), came to Port Townsend in 1882 as vicar of St. Paul's church. Shortly thereafter, he built this residence which seems to make an architectural statement anticipating Rupert Brooke's lines "...there's some corner of a foreign field that is forever England." Victorian architecture, frequently more romantic than practical, sought token inspiration from such sources as ruined abbeys, dramatically sited castles or picturesque fortifications. The Reverend Alexander's "castle" was modest in scale and somewhat awkward in its proportions. Its crenelated tower was designed as a cistern to catch rainwater—supposedly to assure the vicar of plentiful bath water. The whimsy of the conception is appealing and one is tempted to speculate that the supply of bricks used in the tower forced later economies in the scale of the living quarters. The stress on symmetry seems curiously alien to memoried battlements that the builder must have attempted to evoke.

Alexander's Castle, Fort Worden

Capt. R.W. deLion house - 1883

Capt. deLion

DeLion was a Bavarian descendant of a French family. He spoke seven languages and lived in Chile for twenty years before coming to Port Townsend, where he entered the shipping and commission business. This house was his second in Port Townsend, and the December 27, 1883 **Weekly Argus** describes it as follows:

The main building is 40x40 feet and the L 20x24, and 25 feet in the clear. It has a square French roof. The whole building throughout is hard finished and elaborately ornamented with cornices and center pieces. Double bay windows extend from floor to roof on both sides. These windows are ornamented inside with arches and statuettes. The dining room is 25x18 feet and the sitting room 22x18. The whole house is heated by a furnace in the cellar. The foundation is of stone, 22 inches wide, and the cellar is entirely of the same material. The fittings inside include all the modern conveniences.

It reportedly cost $9,000, probably the most expensive house in Port Townsend at the time, and the first with central heating.

DeLion served as consul to Chile and Peru, and as city councilman and mayor. In addition to his thriving shipping and commission business, he opened the deLion and Barthrop Company, which dealt in paint and building materials.

He also built a huge drydock which was to aid Port Townsend's shipbuilding industry. The Puget Sound Drydock Company, of which he was president, asked the town for a $50,000 bonus to build the 100'x325' drydock. It required two million board feet of lumber and displaced 8,000 tons, making it by far the largest drydock on the Puget Sound. The **Morning Leader** estimated that it would bring Port Townsend $1,000,000 annually in wages and money spent by crews of the ships being repaired. Unfortunately, by the time it was launched in

Capt. R.W. deLion house

October, 1891, Port Townsend's future was clouded by the failure of the railroad deal, and the drydock was towed to Quartermaster Harbor near Tacoma.

DeLion lost a considerable amount of money in the drydock and real estate deals, and a long-term illness had resulted in his frequent use of morphine. He was serving as the Chilean consul in Tacoma when his family felt that he had become dangerous and charged him with insanity. An elaborate and sensational trial followed in November, 1893. The key incident was a struggle at the Keeley Institute in Seattle, where both Capt. and Mrs. deLion were seeking a cure for morphine addiction. Mrs. deLion said that her husband had accused her of unfaithfulness, and attacked her. Capt. deLion said that the struggle was over Mrs. deLion's morphine syringe. He then wrote to his wife stating that he felt that her habit was incurable, and that he wanted a divorce. The jury scrutinized evidence and opinions of several witnesses. Capt. deLion claimed that his children were trying to poison him with a cocaine-laced apple cake, and his children claimed that he tried to give them morphine for minor ailments. Capt. deLion's business dealings came under attack as irrational, but he responded that he had assets of $85,000 and debts of only $5,000. After three votes, the jury decided that, on the evidence of his amazing knowledge of drugs, and his level-headed demeanor during the trial, he was not insane. His wife then filed a claim of community interest. In January, Capt. deLion made out a will, later revised, and on February 24, 1894, he shot himself through the head. He was penniless and left his wife and seven children absolutely without means.

Though the deLion house has undergone some modifications—small paned window sash has replaced the original double-hung sash and shingles have replaced the original clapboard siding—it is the one instance of Port Townsend "improvements" that has been tasteful and benign rather than destructive.

The sedately handsome Italianate house, symmetrical in composition and with a low hipped roof almost invisible at street level, is a classic example of self-containment and restraint. Eschewing the sometimes orgiastic display of decoration that accompanies Italianate Villa architecture, the impact of this house is dependent upon the classic proportions of the Federal and Greek Revival era and condescends to current fashion only in the brackets of the cornice and the slightly more vertical proportions of the window openings. Though shingled exterior walls were rarely, if ever, used in Northwest architecture in this stylistic period, it was an acceptable surfacing material in New England towns at the time. Its use here gives an appropriately "Nantucket" aura to this fine house.

Corbels, R.W. deLion house.

Frank Bartlett house - 1883

Port Townsend's **Morning Leader** summarized Frank Bartlett's career in the February 25, 1890 edition: "Frank A. Bartlett, Acting mayor of Port Townsend during the absence of Hon. J.A. Kuhn at the State legislature, came to this city from his native state, Maine, nearly 30 years ago...From a bashful youth he has grown and developed into the general manager and equal partner of the largest mercantile establishment on the lower Puget Sound...Mr. Bartlett is well attached to his business and is reckoned one of the wealthiest men of Jefferson County".

At the age of twenty-four and already married and manager of the business, Bartlett built this house, which reputedly cost $6,000, one of the most expensive houses in the city at the time. He was Director of the Port Townsend Mill Co. and later president of the Steel Wire and Nail Co. Following the depression and the dissolution of C.C. Bartlett and Co. he moved to a less auspicious house and became a "Gents Furnisher".

The Bartlett house, along with the Starrett house, has deservedly acquired national significance. The mansard roof in American architecture was not a rarity. Almost immediately following its revival in Second Empire Paris it had crossed the Atlantic and was used on houses, schools, business and banking establishments as well as public buildings. Often used badly and grafted awkwardly onto structures ill-proportioned for its massive superstructure, by the 1880s it had already begun to wane as a modish style on the eastern seaboard. The particular significance of the Bartlett house is that the anonymous architect has solved an almost insuperable problem: designing a formal two-story cottage of quite humble proportions that jauntily supports a mansard roof without being crushed by its visual weight.

Frank A. Bartlett house, end of Polk near Jefferson

The success of the design, resulting in an almost doll-house charm, is due to the skillful proportions and solidity of the concept. The thin and often attenuated forms of Victorian construction in wood are hardly capable of supporting the same massive roofs that adorned the stone town houses and hotels of Paris. The Bartlett house proportions have been intentionally broadened. The bays are wide and substantial with their Italianate detailing, and it lacks the weightless quality so often felt in wooden construction. Only the pavilion-like porch seems relatively without weight, but since it projects forward and free of a supporting function, its roof is flat, and it can be treated more playfully. The porch along the cliff side was originally unenclosed and the color scheme would have been somber and perhaps in contrasting tones. Otherwise the house survives remarkably intact and a tribute to how stylishly the Victorians were capable of building.

Capt. Charles Sawyer house -1887

Originally located across Jefferson Street from the Rothschild house, this house was built by contractor William McCurdy for Mary Webster as a rental establishment. When the city decided to lower Jefferson Street to improve access, the house was sold to Capt. Charles Sawyer, who moved it to its present location in 1890 and occupied it. It was comparatively easy to move houses in the Victorian era. The absence of overhead wiring and the relatively light weight of the frame structures made it possible to jack them up, place hardwood rollers beneath them, and with teams of horses or oxen, move them to more desirable sites.

The Sawyer house is seen to best advantage from the grounds of the Bell Tower where the porch combines with the elegantly detailed bay to form a striking asymmetrical composition unusually compact and substantial in frame houses. The ability of Victorian architects and builders to give small houses an aura of solidity and importance is demonstrated in this finely proportioned house that utilizes the stock decorative accessories then available. Brackets, panels, and columns are incorporated into a Villa-style house made even more substantial by the visual "weight" of the mansard roof. Though many of the details seem to have been inspired or reinterpreted from the earlier Frank A. Bartlett house, it is by no means entirely imitative. In some ways this house is the more typical Victorian-style of the decade both in its asymmetry and in its more vertical window and door proportions. The profile of its mansard roof has less "flare" than the Frank A. Bartlett house. The interior floor plan was a standard arrangement for a small house and the stair and moulding details are stock items.

Capt. Charles Sawyer's house.

Capt. Thomas Grant house - 1887

Capt. Grant, born of Scottish parents in Pugwash, Nova Scotia, in 1851, arrived in the Puget Sound in 1874. He spent most of his life on the sea, commanding, piloting, and owning various boats. His wealth seemed to fluctuate, due to the nature of the shipping business. He probably built this house during one of his periods of relative prosperity.

The generous scale of the house and the particularly fine two-story symmetrical bays—widely spaced and richly detailed—would indicate that this, unlike many of Port Townsend's frame structures, was architecturally designed. The Italianate Villa, of which this is an exceptional example, stressed self-containment. The roof forms were inconspicuous or invisible and the bracketed cornice gave weight and finality to the exterior walls. The articulation of the corners by both color and projection are typical. As larger panes of glass became available, the pragmatic Victorian builders increased window sizes and expanded the size of bays, making such houses as this light and sunny. Though often the preconceived desire for symmetry on the exterior froze the interior plan into uncompromising matched parlors to the right and left of a central hall, the plan in this instance is asymmetrical and fluid, allowing a generous high-ceilinged parlor and sitting rooms to the left, as well as more intimate closed spaces to the right.

Capt. Thomas Grant house, Lincoln and Pierce

George Starrett house -1889

George E. Starrett arrived from Thomaston, Maine in the early 1880s in his late 20s. It was during Port Townsend's building boom, and he quickly established himself as a carpenter, builder, contractor, and brick manufacturer on the east end of Water Street, close to the sawmill at Point Hudson, which he later operated. In 1889, he made a statement to the **Leader** that he had built 350 houses in Port Townsend (or roughly one a week since his arrival) and was building his own residence at a cost of $6,000.

The house, built to exemplify his profession, was a gift to his wife of two years, the former Ann van Bokkelen, daughter of one of the town's more colorful and prominent pioneers, John J.H. van Bokkelen.

The architecture of the Starrett house is truly remarkable in the originality of its concept and the successful integration of diverse elements into an imposing and harmonious mass which make it—more than any other Port Townsend house—not only of local but of national significance.

By the late nineteenth century the Stick Style had become one of a series of sub-styles from which builders might borrow elements, but its origins extended back to the mid-century when architects such as Wheeler and Richardson were searching for a less romantic and more honestly structural approach to building. It is rare to find Stick Style elements surviving into the last decades of the century other than as decorative features. But in the Starrett house we see a strong emphasis on structural clarity on the exterior of the building. In fact, the vertical articulation of the edges of the tower and bays, juxtaposed against the horizontal banding that emphasizes the stacking of the interior floors, becomes a most satisfying exterior diagram of the structure.

Essentially the house celebrates the inherent qualities of sawn wood and the repetition of the angular forms of the window pediments, repeated in the roof gables, gives it an honesty and consistency of expression almost unique in late Victorian architecture in the west.

The symmetry of the two wings that flank the great stair tower is alleviated by carefully studied asymmetry in the window bay projections and gable barge-board ornamentation.

Though the overall dramatic impact of the profile is an element of Queen Anne-style intention, Queen Anne eccentricities of massing and the arbitrary juxtaposition of various materials and textures has given way to an inherent sense of harmony and order that would be even more apparent were the original contrasting green and light green paint scheme restored.

The exterior is surprisingly free of applied ornament and eschews lathe-turned decoration, spools and spindles, in favor of more architectural decorative elements. The ten-room interior, however, is heavily ornamented with elaborated moldings, and on the door and window entablatures are corner medallions carved with lions, doves and ferns. Some of the ceilings and walls are adorned with stenciled decoration and paintings.

The tower is an ornament itself. S.H. Shanks completed the elaborate free-hung stairway on April 20, 1890. On the ceiling of the tower are George Chapman's painted allegorical figures of the four seasons. Local society apparently objected to the "lewd" painting of Winter, and some criticized the Starretts for having it in their house.

Neither widows' walks nor lookout towers were common features in western seaside architecture. Though the 1883 Flavel house in Astoria, Oregon, had an imposing tower with Italianate detailing, it is not so skillfully incorporated into the fabric of the structure nor so sculpturally conceived as the Starrett tower. It is more likely that George Starrett's conception came from prototypes in Maine.

What seems a curious omission, the lack of fireplaces in the house, was hardly done as a measure of economy. Their very absence in a late nineteenth century house served to impress on any observant visitor that such "antiquated" heating devices had been eliminated in favor of stoves and central heating.

Interior of tower, George Starrett house showing "The Four Seasons".

Henry Wylie house -1889

This house, described briefly by the January 1, 1890 **Morning Leader** as a "very pretty Queen Anne," was built for Henry Wylie and his wife Claribel for $2,000. He was employed as a civil engineer and county surveyor.

Of the many small vernacular houses in Port Townsend, this undoubtedly is one of the most consistent in style and most harmoniously restored. Only the enclosure of a rear porch and the addition of a dormer window have altered the original appearance. It would be a natural assumption that Wylie had had some architectural background in his training as a civil engineer. It was a progressive design for the late 1880s and surprisingly eschews almost all the stock decorative details, mass produced at the time, and seems to exemplify a current architectural trend toward more "honest" decorative effects that were derived from structure and sheathing. Such functional decoration and restraint are seen to better advantage in this cottage than in the more pretentious Queen Anne houses in the city.

Wylie house, Lincoln and Van Buren Sts.

Elias Devoe house -1888

Elias W. Devoe

Elias Devoe was a partner of C.P. Wakeman and Co., a contracting firm that did most of the masonry work in Port Townsend during the boom, including several downtown buildings and a $25,927 contract for the basement and walls of the Customs House. He had George Starrett build this house, and to show his company's skill, he veneered the house in brick. Since the local brick was soft, it was stuccoed to protect it from the weather, and to show that the exterior was actually brick, the red stucco had raised and painted ridges to represent the mortar between the bricks. A 3,000 gallon water tower, which has been torn down, used to supply several homes in the area, but the carriage house, though moved, still survives. Devoe sold the house only a few years after he built it, and A.I. Smith became the owner in 1893 when he foreclosed on the mortgage.

This fashionable and archetypal Queen Anne residence must have set new standards of taste in Port Townsend at a time when bracketed Villa-style architecture was the norm. Devoe's desire to exploit brick in a dazzling residence was better served by the Queen Anne style, with its wide latitude in the use of varying textures and materials, than by the more sedate Italianate or Second Empire forms of Villa architecture. Though the house is grand in scale and has a monumentality unique in Port Townsend residences, there is a disarming and sometimes alarming whimsy and lack of sophistication in the application of ornament. The two-story bay has a curious inconsistency in the window proportions and a disturbing break in continuity between the first and second floors. The superfluity of ornament piled on top of the gabled bay has a certain barbaric appeal but also is patently top-heavy. Though not so refined in subtleties of taste and proportion as the Starrett or Bartlett houses, the initial impact of this awesome home is one of almost Byzantine splendor.

Elias Devoe house

Albert C. Adams house -1889

The Adams house was one of the larger homes to be built for speculation rather than for the actual occupation by the owner. Albert C. Adams was the owner, but Capt. John Quincy Adams held the mortgage on the $5,000 house. The 1890 directory lists them as capitalists and shows that their home was a few blocks away. Albert C. Adams owned extensive property at the time and was a real estate speculator and builder.

The actual residents of the house in 1890 were George B. Hinds and Edward S. Campbell of E.S. Campbell and Co., a real estate and insurance firm. Campbell and J.W. Hinds (a third resident who was also chaplain of the Seaman's Bethel) were secretary and vice president, respectively, of the Marine Savings and Loan. D.T. Denny, of Seattle, was president. It opened November 1, 1890 in the Mount Baker Block, just twenty-four days before the Oregon Improvement Company's railroad project went into receivership, signalling the end of the boom for Port Townsend. The bank was one of the four that did not survive the ensuing depression.

There were also at least five roomers and one domestic living in the house at one time. Although building was going on at a frantic rate, the influx of people in the late 1880s produced a housing shortage and roomers were taken into many homes.

Eventually Adams, too, was striken by the depression, and he lost the house when the First National Bank foreclosed on a mortgage.

The architecture of the house partakes of elements borrowed from three concurrent sub-styles of Victorian architecture: the Bracketed Villa Style, Queen Anne, and Stick Style. Though the

Albert C. Adams house, Tyler and F Sts.

prominent gables and dramatic turret dominate the ensemble and are purely Queen Anne, the plain surface textures of the exterior walls and the consistent shape and proportion of the severe bracketed windows are Villa Style. Perhaps because it was built for speculation it has a relatively modest amount of decorative details for the period. The resulting uncluttered angularity seems a positive attribute today and despite its hybrid origins, the generous scale and striking profile are undeniably impressive.

Albert C. Adams house ceiling medallion.

Lucinda Hastings house - 1890

Lucinda Hastings

As the wife of Loren Brown Hastings, Lucinda was the only person to live through, and participate in, the entire early history of the town. Most of the early pioneers died during the 1880s, shortly before the boom period when anticipation that Port Townsend would be the great port of the Puget Sound area seemed to be materializing. She arrived in 1852, the first white woman in the area, survived Indian wars and eked out a subsistence in the wilderness. She saw the town prosper with the promise of a railroad, and watched the dreams fade in the depression of 1891. (See Hastings Building.)

The **Morning Leader** in January 1891 described the new house:

Of the fine residences recently built, that of Mrs. Lucinda Hastings is the most costly yet built in this city, representing an investment of nearly $14,000. It is two stories, occupies a commanding view and is admirably arranged throughout...

The entire building is heated with hot water, which is probably the first house in town to adopt this new feature. There are, however, five beautiful and cosy fireplaces. In these latter and in the stairway is displayed some of the very excellent work done at the Hastings Lumber and Manufacturing Company's mill. The fireplace in the parlor is finished in oak, ornamented with some of the most handsome designs. The stairway is solid oak, and is a thing of beauty. The newells are tastefully carved and ornamented. Those at the approach of the stairs are carved so as to represent the most perfect oak leaves, acorns, etc., the newell post being surmounted with the imitation of a mammoth acorn. The stairway is lighted by three windows of jewel glass at the first landing, the center one of which represents "Morning and Night," the other two are of conventional pattern. Mr. Charles

Lucinda Hastings house, Franklin and Munroe Sts.

Packard, who built the house, and who is also superintendent of the Hastings Manufacturing Company, at whose mill all of the interior work of the building was designed and made, has certainly in this admirably sustained his reputation for fine work.

Though large and commodious, the Hastings house is more interesting for its decorative features and its historic associations than for architectural qualities. The contractor obviously thought, as did many Victorian builders, that a house was a comfortable assemblage of parts. Using a large and somewhat cumbersome framework not substantially different from a farmhouse, Packard assembled a wealth of rich interior details in oak and applied to the exterior the customary brackets and spindles associated with Victorian well-being. The Queen Anne style, which began to supercede the Villa styles of the previous decades in popularity, is introduced hesitatingly in the bands of decorative shingles and in the diagonal juxtaposition of the entry. Well-maintained and commanding in scale and siting, it was undoubtedly an object of personal as well as civic pride: a fitting residence for Port Townsend's most vital and legendary woman.

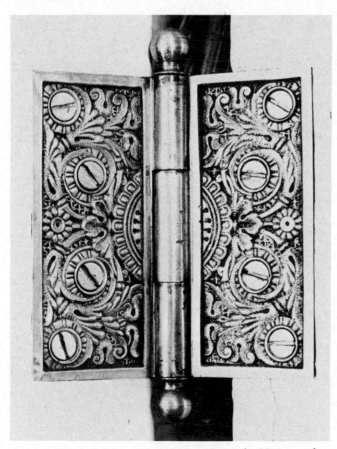 

Lucinda Hastings house, door fixtures.

Frank Hastings house -1890

Frank Hastings

Born in Portland in 1848, Frank Hastings moved to Port Townsend with his father, Loren B. Hastings, in 1852. He was educated in local schools and the Territorial University in Seattle. When his father retired, Frank and his brother, Oregon, operated the mercantile business and eventually sold it to C.C. Bartlett. He operated the first commission business in Port Townsend, but sold that to concentrate on real estate investment in 1888 as the boom was starting to build. In 1890, he was considered, at least by the **Morning Leader**, to be "a man in the prime of life and a true specimen of Washington's best manhood", who "has made a comfortable fortune in the Key City and now is a gentleman of leisure". In that year he was president of the Electric Street Railway, Power, and Light, heavily invested in real estate and the Hastings Lumber and Manufacturing Company, and elected as state senator.

Hastings planned to build a $10,000 house opposite the residence of his brother-in-law, D.W. Littlefield. The exterior was completed during the summer of 1890, but that winter the depression caused a drastic decrease in real estate prices and investment, and although work continued he was unable to finish the house. The kitchen, dining room, and one living room were finished, but in the rest of the house, there were no windows, stairs, plastered walls or finished floors.

C.A. Olson purchased the shell for $2,500 at a county sale in 1904, including six lots and a large carriage house. Olson could not obtain the original blueprints, so he and Julius Sather finished the house as well as they could without them.

In 1911, the headquarters for the customs district were moved to Seattle, and August Duddenhausen, a Civil War pensioner in his 70s and former city clerk and deputy treasurer, who was rooming with the

Frank W. Hastings house, Walker and Washington Sts.

Olsons, was asked by the German Consul to handle minor affairs in Port Townsend. For a year and a half he transacted some official business at the Olson's house and seemingly forever established it as the legendary "German Consulate".

The Frank Hastings house, unlike the Lucinda Hastings or F.W. James houses which made tentative compromise efforts to incorporate elements of the increasingly fashionable Queen Anne style, is a consistent and bravura expression of that final eclectic phase of Victorian architecture. Though having little to do with any actual historic style, the "Queen Anne" is usually traced to the Philadelphia Centennial Exposition of 1876 and the British Pavilions there which had a powerful impact on American architects, breaking the conservative historicism of academic architecture. Not only did this fashionable new mode of building encourage a greater diversity of materials, it allowed for a far less formal arrangement of interior spaces. The static compartmentalized rooms gave way to a more fluid plan, the entry hall became larger and more important, and rooms could be sized and juxtaposed according to actual use rather than arbi-

Frank W. Hastings house, detail

trarily filling out the corner of a preconceived square or rectangular floor plan. Concurrently, American social mores were becoming more relaxed and the less formal architecture coincided with less rigid social expectations in a mutually dependent evolution. All the elements of a full-bodied Queen Anne style are seen in the house: the variety of materials—shingles, brick and clapboard, the asymmetry and dramatization of roof forms, and the extension of architectural forms into space. The last is particularly apparent. The asymmetrical towers and chimney extending upward and the porch and widely cantilevered eaves extending outward begin to relate interior and exterior space as mutually inter-dependent: an early manifestation of indoor-outdoor living. Though the asymmetry of forms gives the house a casual quality, there is a studied inter-action of the parts and a consistency in proportion that sets this house apart from other Port Townsend residential architecture of the same period. The delay in completing the interiors has resulted in a certain stylistic time lag and the woodwork of the entrance hall and stairway are more sober Edwardian than experimental Queen Anne.

Frank W. Hastings house, tower

James C. Saunders house -1891
architect: Edward A. Batwell

James C. Saunders was a customs collector, president of the Commercial Bank, and speculator in real estate. He arrived in Port Townsend in the late 1880s during the town's period of greatest optimism, and built this large $8,000 house. After his term as customs collector expired in 1898, he lost the house when one of many mortgages was foreclosed, and left town.

Though remodelled on the interior by several owners and serving at one time as a Youth Hostel, the exterior of the house remains substantially as it was built and the interior has a considerable amount of surviving detail, including the five fireplaces that, supplemented by stoves, served to heat the house, although inadequately. The third floor attic, 20 feet high at the apex, is clear of supports and has served as a dance floor, accommodating four squares of square dancers.

Houses of such ambitious scale were not unusual in the late nineteenth century, but seldom is such a medley of styles brought together in one structure as to summarize the conflicting trends of Victorian eclecticism. Port Townsend architect Edward A. Batwell, with offices in the Hastings Building, would have been dependent upon books and publications for knowledge of current trends in architecture—as were most practitioners in the nineteenth century. Here he incorporates many avant garde ideas, not always completely assimilated, into what basically was a house meant to please a conservative provincial businessman. The variety of roof shapes, dramatic chimneys, and porch forms extending into space are characteristic of the Queen Anne style. Because of its accommodation of a flexible interior plan this style had, by the 1890s, generally superceded the more self-contained and inflexible Villa styles of the 1870s and 1880s. Combined with such

James C. Saunders house, Sims Way

characteristic elements of the Queen Anne, however, are elements of the classical revival and the Shingle Style, currently fashionable in eastern resort towns such as Newport, Rhode Island. The shingled planes of wall that curve inward to frame the recessed balcony in the third story gable; the pilasters and pediment that adorn the dormers; and particularly the chaste entablature framing the dining room fireplace with its whimsically placed window anticipate the Colonial Revival as interpreted by McKim, Mead and White.

James C. Saunders house, dining room fireplace.

Peter Mutty house
-1891

Peter Mutty, popular manager of the Discovery Hotel, built this house and settled in Port Townsend in 1891, a time when most people were leaving. In 1892, the city assessed this house higher than either the Starrett or deLion houses in the next block. Mutty sold the house in 1893, but opened Wanamaker and Mutty's, a grain and grocery store, a short time later in the growing shopping area uptown. The store was eventually sold to the Aldrich family.

American technical ingenuity in the nineteenth century was responsible for the greater efficiency of its industrial production over English or European operations and by the final decades of the century assembly line production had replaced older and more time-consuming craft techniques. Decorative and structural architectural elements were one of the products of this industrial evolution and the distinctive appearance of late American Victorian architecture was the result of this phenomenon. In Port Townsend the Mutty house is possibly the best surviving example of how a simple house of inexpensive construction could be transformed by fashionable frivolities applied to the surface. Though the severity of the roof forms suggest an antiquated style harking back to the previous decade, the addition of porches, bays, exterior wainscotting, fishscale shingling, sunburst gable tympanum, and colored window glass transform a bulky and unfashionable house into an acceptable residence for Mutty, the aspiring grocer and grain dealer. The tendency toward complexity in the 1890s was usually more than skin deep. It involved greater fluidity in interior spatial relationships and an attempt to integrate the interior and exterior architectural spaces. Though the house is undoubtedly beguiling, its charm is almost totally the result of its skin-deep decorative scheme which distracts but doesn't camouflage the almost evangelical puritanism of the underlying structure.

Peter Mutty house, Lawrence and Taylor Sts.

Francis Wilcox James house - 1891

In 1853, Francis Wilcox James, an Englishman, arrived in Port Townsend and held several jobs before opening a mercantile business. He was a clerk in the Hastings Company, customs inspector, and keeper of the Cape Flattery Lighthouse. He then opened a store which he sold to C.C. Bartlett in 1866, but later repurchased and operated until he retired in 1882 to devote more time to his private affairs. The failure of the railroad project in 1891 and the following depression didn't seem to impoverish James. He built this house for $10,000 in 1891-2 when there was virtually no other private construction in town, and on his death in 1920 he left an ample fortune.

The **Morning Leader's** reference to the James house as being "Restoration" style must certainly have been a quotation from James himself since the term could have had little meaning to Port Townsendites, who would think of it as Queen Anne. The complexity of roof and chimney forms and the variety of surface textures would have been considered fashionable attributes at the time. The final decade of the nineteenth century was one of rapid transition in American architecture and though the house today looks picturesque and romantic, it was "modern" at the time to the extent that the interior plan determined the exterior architectural forms and convenience outweighed preconceived aesthetic concepts of exterior appearance. Though certain exterior details seem curiously inept, (for example, the fragile, spindly porch that seems inadequate to carry the surmounting shingled parapet) the interior details—for all their contrivance—are richly impressive. Few Port Townsend interiors can rival the variety

Francis Wilcox James house, Harrison and Washington Sts.

and quality of woodwork. The parquet floors and splendid staircase extending through three floors were custom designed for the house. Other interior details, fireplace overmantels and wainscotting were likely stock decorations, but the generous and inventive interior spaces and fine craftmanship were to be a fitting swan song to Port Townsend's age of prosperity.

Francis Wilcox James house, interior details

Charles Eisenbeis house - 1892

Charles Eisenbeis

Charles Eisenbeis, a young Prussian baker, arrived in Port Townsend in 1858. At that time the closest source of supply for ships' bread and crackers was Portland, so Eisenbeis opened the Pioneer Bakery, the first in the State. At one time or another he was involved in a multitude of enterprises in addition to his bakery: a grocery, clothing store, brewery, and a brickyard which supplied materials for many of the downtown buildings. He was Port Townsend's first mayor and was also involved in the lumber mill, bank, the Port Townsend Steel, Wire, and Nail Co. and was instrumental in arranging the contracts to bring the railroad to the city. As holder of major downtown property and partner in a syndicate which held outlying real estate as well as a vast wooden hotel on a hill above the anticipated railway terminal, Eisenbeis was hit more severely by the depression than other local businessmen, and the hotel never opened. However, his tax assessment of $82,525 in 1890 was second only to Lucinda Hastings and his optimism, in spite of the depression, was such that in 1892, with probably the last bricks that his yard produced, he undertook the construction of a monumental house reminiscent of his homeland.

Manresa Hall, a name that later evolved into Manresa Castle, was the name given to the property in 1925 when it was purchased by the Jesuit Order as a retreat. It was enlarged at that time and the original turreted portion of the house had stucco surfacing applied to the brick.

American periodicals in the last quarter of the nineteenth century had begun to exploit a taste for dramatic scenery, exotic lands, and romantic architecture. Undoubtedly Eisenbeis' instructions to his contractor and architect, A.S. Whiteway, were to create the

Charles Eisenbeis house (Manresa Hall), Cleveland and 7th Sts.

semblance of a medieval Prussian castle. The request was not extra-ordinary at the time. Eclecticism in American architecture following the Civil War was burgeoning and historic architecture was considered a resource to be exploited. Any architect trained under the beaux art system would, within reason, be prepared to honor a client's request to capture the spirit of the Alhambra or reproduce the essence of the fortifications at Carcasonne.

Though sadly deprived of its original texture and warmth at the time of its remodelling by the Jesuits, the dynamic asymmetry of the castellated structure with the sculptural forms of roof and dormers silhouetted against the sky, must have epitomized for Eisenbeis the ultimate symbol of success: a humble baker risen to chatelain of a castle.

Eisenbeis house from west side.

160

Charles Eisenbeis house, details

Miscellaneous
Structures

Bell Tower - 1890

In late 1889, the fire department was in need of two things: an engine house for their new $900 chemical engine, and a bell that D.H. Hill's "fire boys" could hear to alert volunteers. At the suggestion of Hill, the son of N.D. Hill and Port Townsend's firechief for many years, these were combined in a structure which was built on the Tyler Street right-of-way at the top of the bluff. This location enabled the fire department to avoid scaling the steep grades every time there was a fire uptown. The January 1, 1890 **Morning Leader** reported:

The contract has been let for a new engine house for the chemical engine, and bell-tower on Tyler and Jefferson Streets. The bell-tower will be 50 feet high, and it is presumed by the thinking part of the community that an electric light will be suspended from the lofty superstructure which, being on the hill, will show to splendid advantage.

This unique and dynamic structure, at the time it was built, could hardly have been considered "architecture". The only condescension to fashion was the use of decorative brackets at the corners of the roof. The acute batter of the walls and superstructure give a pyramidal profile to the construction and though undoubtedly done as a bracing device to counteract the strong winds, it endows the forthright little tower with a structural honesty and an engaging eccentricity far removed from the self-conscious eclectically decorated formal architecture of the era.

Bell Tower, Jefferson and Tyler Sts.

165

Chetzemoka Park -1905

*Chetzemoka &
Queen Victoria*

In 1905, the Civic Improvement Club took on their first big project, a five-acre park on the "outskirts" of the city on the land that the city had bought for that purpose two years before. They organized a work day, and on June 11, 1905, stores closed and several people gathered to clear out debris and underbrush. A picnic dinner was served at noon and the day turned out to be more festive than arduous. After the initial effort, work continued on the park in the same low-budget, volunteer-labor manner. The bandstand was built and the Fort band played on Sundays during the summer. By December the principal roadways and paths had been graded and cindered. A roadway had been laid to the beach, and benches and seats had been placed about the park. Up to that time only $600 had been expended, plus $135 to purchase an additional acre, and the major work had been done. Eventually a small zoo, stone fireplaces, and long tables were added. It was named Chetzemoka Park after the Clallam Indian Chief who had been so instrumental to the success of the early pioneers.

The appearance of the park is so typical and endemic to the Northwest that only visitors alien to the area would be aware of the unique and positive qualities that it contains. Stands of Douglas fir in their native state are never seen without heavy undergrowth of salal, huckleberry, and vine maple. As the firs mature, the deep shade beneath causes them to reach for light and shed their lower branches. Once the undergrowth is cleared by man, the sheer unencumbered vertical thrust of the trunks and the very high canopy of shade overhead filters the sun and alters the quality of light. Such groves of fir as this contain only space overhead and horizontal space is boundless

Band stand at Chetzemoka Park.

and extends across the straits. Fussy flower beds and ill-conceived "improvements" at one's feet are distracting and only the Edwardian bandstand seems appropriate in scale and free of cliche. The semi-tamed forest setting carpeted by lawn and with wonderful views framed by the sequence of vertical divisions give the small park a breathtaking spatial quality too easily taken for granted.

Haller Fountain
- dedicated 1906

On Labor Day, September 3, 1906, one thousand people anxiously awaited the arrival of the steamer **Indianapolis**. It carried Theodore N. Haller and assorted dignitaries who were coming to dedicate the new statue at the foot of the stairs at the intersection of Washington and Taylor Streets. Upon Haller's arrival, two hours late, the Sixth Artillery Band played, and the dignitaries were escorted two blocks to the site.

Haller was the son of Granville Haller, who constructed and commanded Fort Townsend. Granville was in charge of protecting the settlers and local Indians from hostile Indian attacks from 1856 to 1860. Both Theodore and his brother, Morris, were prominent in Port Townsend, but later moved to Seattle. Theodore dedicated the fountain to the early pioneers, particularly his father and brother. After Haller's speech, a poem about Galatea was recited (no one seems sure why the statue was renamed Galatea), and everyone promptly adjourned to the new Chetzemoka park, where the Elks picnic lasted well into the night.

After the initial indignity of being dedicated two hours late, the fountain suffered a variety of abuses. It was used for shows by Charlie Lange's jumping trout. Soldiers used to pose with the statue for gag pictures until it eventually tumbled and was stored for some time to prevent further damage. The fountain became a receptacle for bottles and litter until it was filled in with dirt and planted. It was later dug out and restored to its original use as a fountain.

Though the central figure may seem overly sentimental to a twentieth century observer, it is a mark of tolerance, sophistication, or resignation that such a display of unabashed voluptuousness would be acceptable to a Port Townsend audience in the 1906 Edwardian era. Its origins are somewhat earlier, dating back at least to 1875, when it

appeared in the catalog for The Mott Iron Works of New York under the title "Venus, Rising from the Sea." It later appeared as "Innocence" at the World Columbian Exposition of 1893 in Chicago. It was displayed at the Mexican exhibition in the Horticultural Building. The fountain elicited extravagant contemporary comment: "...sequestered among the luxuriant foliage of Mexico is a specimen of rare merit...a fountain design which is well-calculated by its gracefulness to enchain the instant attention of a visitor and to invite extravagant plaudits of admiration."

The European inspiration for the figure is not difficult to isolate since United States puritanism strongly dictated against such overtly erotic sculpture. American sculptors might occasionally conceive of Liberty clothed in a somewhat disheveled wardrobe, but less often than Europeans turned to unclad mythical images as subject matter. Sculptural images in America were more often conceived as didactic images allegorically illustrating the Virtues and one might suspect that the citizens of Port Townsend, had they been given a choice, would have opted for Chastity. Motherhood, Hope, or Charity.

Victorian sculptors universally favored the dramatic moment frozen in time and often exploited such rococo compositions as this—heavily endowed with sentimentality. The reaction against such artificiality set in during the 1920s and has persisted for a half century. The statue has survived quite miraculously the disfavor and indignities of a more pragmatic age. In this contemporary era, when a re-examination of all our inherited prejudices is taking place, she may find a future audience less blase.

Point Wilson Lighthouse -1914

At the request of Puget Sound shippers, the government built the original Point Wilson lighthouse in 1879. The first structure was a white keeper's house surmounted by a large square tower with an oil lamp for a light. D.H. Littlefield, who married into the Hastings family, was the original lighthouse keeper. The present lighthouse was built in 1914 and an electric light was installed at that time.

The spartan image of the Point Wilson Lighthouse, enhanced by its site so spare of foliage, contrasts emphatically with the Victorian gentilities and verdure of the nineteenth century townsite. There was always a double standard for Victorian architecture. One standard, dominated by a preoccupation with style and fashion, was applied to houses, hotels, civic and commercial architecture. Other architecture —factories, barns, trainsheds, lighthouses, (and in Port Townsend, the Bell Tower),were considered purely as functional necessities and consequently freed from any obligatory decorative or stylistic enrichment.

This dual standard survived well into the twentieth century until eventually Frank Lloyd Wright's philosophy—if not practice—of treating the house also as a functional organism, set a more universal standard. The Point Wilson Lighthouse is patently conceived of in purely functional terms. The housing for the lighthouse keeper, the storage dependencies, and the tower itself—faceted to reduce wind pressure—are singularly unaffected by current considerations of fashion. Lighthouse architecture, a comparatively rare type of building, evolved more slowly than other historical architectural forms due to the immutable function that it served. Consequently, the similarities between an eighteenth century lighthouse in New England or on

Point Wilson Lighthouse, Fort Worden

the coast of Cornwall and a twentieth century lighthouse on Puget Sound are more striking than are the differences. Such architecture, forming an exclamation mark on sites dramatic even without embellishment, has long had romantic connotations that were reflected in western literature and art. The obsolescence of their function due to modern navigational sophistication has regrettably eliminated forever this dramatic genre of architecture from the coastlines of the world.

Bibliography

Evening Call, The, September 18, 1903, Port Townsend

Gibbs, Jim **West Coast Lighthouses**, Superior Publishing Co., Seattle 1974

Hines, Rev. H.K. **An Illustrated History of the State of Washington,** The Lewis Publishing Company, Chicago 1893

History of the First Presbyterian Church, pamphlet, 1948

Hunt, Dorothy, applications to the **National Register of Historic Places,** prepared by Dorothy Hunt

Jefferson County Historical Society, **With Pride in Heritage**, Professional Publishing Company, Portland, Oregon 1966

McCurdy, James G. **By Juan de Fuca's Strait**, Metropolitan Press, Portland, Oregon 1937

McDonald, Betty, **The Egg and I**, Lippincot, Philadelphia 1945

McDonald, Lucille and Lenggenhager, Werner **Where the Washingtonians Lived**, Superior Publishing Company, Seattle 1969

North Pacific History Company **History of the Pacific Northwest**, vols. I and II, Portland, Oregon 1889

Pacific Fisherman, Aug. 1931

Polk, L.B. & Co. **Olympia, Port Townsend, Fairhaven, New Whatcom Directory 1890**, Detroit 1890 (also 1897 and various subsequent years)

Port Townsend Illustrated, Leader Publishing Co., Port Townsend 1890

Port Townsend Leader (Weekly Leader, Morning Leader), entire file, especially October 2, 1889 - January 1, 1891, January 1, 1892, Leader Publishing Company, Port Townsend, Washington

Rothschild house pamphlet

Simpson, Jerry, **Victorian Port Townsend,** pamphlet, 1961

Smith, May B., **Picturesque Port Townsend,** unpublished manuscript, 1929

Speidel, William, **Sons of the Profits** Nettle Creek Press, Seattle

Washington Standard, Olympia, Washington, May 9, 1874

Welch, William D. **A Brief Historical Sketch of Port Townsend,** Crown Zellerbach, Port Townsend Mill, and Port Townsend Chamber of Commerce 1941

West Shore, The, Portland, Oregon, May, 1885

Willison, Nelly Frances, **History of Little Old St. Paul's**, pamphlet

Index

Printed in Canada